CROSS SEEKERS™

CrossSeekers:
Discipleship Covenant for
a New Generation

" You will seek me and find me
when you seek me with all your heart."
Jeremiah 29:13

Editor: Art Herron

Production Specialist: Leanne B. Adams

Graphic Designer: Bob Redden

Printed in the United States of America

ISBN 0-7673-9084-9

Table of Contents

About the Writers...

Bill Henry, writer of chapter one, is Director of National Student Ministry at LifeWay Christian Resources of the Southern Baptist Convention.

Previously, he was Associate Director of National Student Ministry. For 12 years before coming to LifeWay, Henry worked as Associate Director for the Dapartment of Student Work for the Tennessee Baptist Convention.

A native of Nashville, Henry holds a B.S. in business administration and management from Belmont University and a Ph.D. in higher education from Vanderbilt University. He also attended The Southern Baptist Theological Seminary, Louisville, KY.

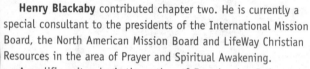

Henry Blackaby contributed chapter two. He is currently a special consultant to the presidents of the International Mission Board, the North American Mission Board and LifeWay Christian Resources in the area of Prayer and Spiritual Awakening.

A prolific writer, he is the author of *Experiencing God: Knowing and Doing the Will of God; Fresh Encounter: God's Pattern for Revival and Spiritual Awakening; Called and Accountable; What the Spirit Is Saying to the Church; When God Speaks;* co-author (with son Richard) of both *How to Recognize God's Voice and Respond in Obedience* and *God's Invitation: A Challenge to College Students.*

Henry Blackaby enjoys working with college students and is a popular speaker at collegiate meetings. He grew up in Canada and earned a B.A. from the University of British Columbia. He earned his B.Div. and Th.M. from Golden Gate Baptist Theological Seminary and a D.D. from Hardin-Simmons University.

Richard Blackaby is author for the remainder of this book. Currently president of the Canadian Southern Baptist Theological Seminary in Cochrane, Alberta, Canada, he has worked extensively with college students and student leaders. Previously, he was a church pastor.

Richard Blackaby graduated from the University of Saskatchewan and earned an M.Div. and a Ph.D. from Southwestern Baptist Theological Seminary.

He is co-author of *God's Invitation: A Challenge to College Students* and *When God Speaks: How to Recognize God's Voice and Respond in Obedience,* both written with his father.

A sought-after speaker for collegiate conferences, he has counseled with many college students considering God's call upon their lives to full-time Christian service.

How to Use this Book

Welcome to the CrossSeekers world. It is a world filled with excitement, hard work, love, accountability, sharing, commitment, adjustments, and spiritual seeking! Who would want to be a part of this type world? Imagine, if you will, a group of young adults committed to seeking the cross of Christ. . .and committed to the life principles found at the foot of the cross. Because this book is in your hand, you may be one of the persons we are talking about.

CrossSeekers is an exciting movement of God within the lives of college students and young adults. It touches into the lives of those who are presently high school juniors and seniors. Continuing through the next nine chapters challenges you to transform *what you say you believe* into a *reality* in lifestyle living. Each chapter moves closer to the cross of Jesus Christ. Reading this book is part of a spiritual journey. The reality is, you will never be *too close* to the cross. The excitement of the journey to the cross never ends.

CrossSeekers are students who have committed their lives to the six principles of the CrossSeekers Covenant. The principles, with a brief description, can be found on the following page. Bottom line—be authentic in your relationship to Scripture and in your relationship with Jesus Christ.

This resource can be used in a variety of ways.

First, it can be used for personal spiritual growth. This is the foundational book for becoming a CrossSeeker. In the privacy of your own room, you can work through this book. The interactive suggestions (indicated with a color screen) will strongly reinforce the learning experience.

Second, it can be used as a group study in your church or campus religious organization during a structured time of Bible study. If your group desires to be known as a CrossSeekers group, this book should be provided for each student to read. At the back of the book, leaders will find "Teaching Helps."

Third, it can be used independently by a group of students who desire to form their own CrossSeekers group on campus. Again, each student should have a copy of this book to read and work through. Additional resources will be available throughout the year.

Already campus groups such as Baptist Collegiate Ministry and Fellowship of Christian Athletes are using this material and the CrossSeekers emphasis to help students grow spiritually. In some instances, it has become the main discipleship program for these groups.

However you choose to use this book, keep seeking the cross of Jesus Christ!

The CrossSeekers™ Covenant

"You will seek me and find me when you seek me with all your heart."
Jeremiah 29:13

CROSS

SEEKERS

As a seeker of the cross of Christ, I am called to break away from trite, nonchalant, laissez faire Christian living. I accept the challenge to divine daring, to consecrated recklessness for Christ, to devout adventure in the face of ridiculing contemporaries. Created in the image of God and committed to excellence as a disciple of Jesus Christ,

I will be a person of integrity

INTEGRITY

"Do your best to present yourself to God as one approved, a workman who does not need to be ashamed and who correctly handles the word of truth." 2 Timothy 2:15

My attitudes and actions reveal my commitment to live the kind of life Christ modeled for me—to speak the truth in love, to stand firm in my convictions, to be honest and trustworthy.

I will pursue consistent spiritual growth

SPIRITUAL GROWTH

"So then, just as you received Christ Jesus as Lord, continue to live in Him, rooted and built up in Him, strengthened in the faith as you were taught, and overflowing with thankfulness." Colossians 2:6-7

The Christian life is a continuing journey, and I am committed to a consistent, personal relationship with Jesus Christ, to faithful study of His word, and to regular corporate spiritual growth through the ministry of the New Testament church.

I will speak and live a relevant, authentic, and consistent witness

WITNESS

"Always be prepared to give an answer to everyone who asks you to give the reason for the hope that you have." 1 Peter 3:15

I will tell others the story of how Jesus changed my life, and I will seek to live a radically changed life each day. I will share the good news of Jesus Christ with courage and boldness.

I will seek opportunities to serve in Christ's name

SERVICE

"The Spirit of the Lord is on me, because He has anointed me to preach good news to the poor. He has sent me to proclaim freedom for the prisoners and recovery of sight for the blind, to release the oppressed, to proclaim the year of the Lord's favor." Luke 4:18-19

I believe that God desires to draw all people into a loving, redeeming relationship with Him. As His disciple, I will give myself to be His hands to reach others in ministry and missions.

I will honor my body as the temple of God, dedicated to a lifestyle of purity

PURITY

"Do you not know that your body is a temple of the Holy Spirit, who is in you, whom you have received from God? You are not your own; you were bought at a price. Therefore honor God with your body." 1 Corinthians 6:19-20

Following the example of Christ, I will keep my body healthy and strong, avoiding temptations and destructive personal vices. I will honor the gift of life by keeping myself sexually pure and free from addictive drugs.

I will be godly in all things, Christlike in all relationships

CHRISTLIKE RELATIONSHIPS

"Therefore, as God's chosen people, holy and dearly loved, clothe yourselves with compassion, kindness, humility, gentleness, and patience. Bear with each other and forgive what grievances you may have against one another. Forgive as the Lord forgave you. And over all these virtues put on love, which binds them all together in perfect unity." Colossians 3:12-14

In every relationship and in every situation, I will seek to live as Christ would. I will work to heal brokenness, to value each person as a child of God, to avoid petty quarrels and harsh words, to let go of bitterness and resentment that hinder genuine Christian love.

TM

EARNESTLY SEEKING?
by Bill Henry
Director of National Student Ministry

As a seeker of the cross of Christ, I am called to break away from trite, nonchalant, laissez-faire Christian living. I accept the challenge to divine daring, to consecrated recklessness for Christ, to devout adventure in the face of ridiculing contemporaries. I acknowledge I am created in the image of God and committed to excellence as a disciple of Jesus Christ.

Shawn is a basketball player with one mission in life...to go professional. As a student athlete from fall to spring, he has one focus only—the game. He is consumed with the game, watching videos of other teams, working out and shooting hoops. Sure he's good—every game his name headlines the sports section. So he waits for the NBA draft, eagerly waiting, earnestly seeking his lifelong dream.

Tara is a pre-med student trying to get into Duke Medical School. Ever since she was eight, she's wanted to be a pediatrician. She volunteered her summers in high school at the local hospital, and then during spring break her junior year, she traveled to Haiti to work with children. That trip clinched it for her! Every morning she eagerly runs to the post office to check her mailbox, earnestly seeking to find out her future.

What are you earnestly seeking? Circle all that apply, and/or add your own to the list.

fame	recognition	fortune
friends	security	success
life on the edge	relationship with Christ	

As a seeker of the cross of Christ. . .

CrossSeekers is about earnestly seeking a relationship with Jesus Christ. It's about allowing Christ to infuse every aspect of your life with His meaning. Matthew 6:33 talks of earnestly seeking:

> *"But seek first his kingdom and his righteousness, and all these things will be given to you as well."*

In the original language, the verb tense implies continuous action: keep on seeking. So, never stop pursuing a relationship with Jesus Christ.

Another quality about this quest is its timelessness. There are no timetables on seeking and finding. Unlike our culture that is bound by time, seeking and knowing Jesus permeates every minute. This casts new meaning to who you are and what your life is about. Realize as a CrossSeeker, your need for instant gratification is replaced by a commitment to eternal values. Would you agree or disagree? Why? Why not?

_____

_____

CrossSeekers are concerned about being a part of His Kingdom and what they can do to realize it now in their lives. It's not that school isn't important, or athletic achievement, or getting a good job, or finding a mate. *Seeking after Christ's kingdom puts all that in context.* Pursuing these goals is a way to serve Christ and others. They are no longer the means to an end; seeking Jesus Christ and His kingdom is the means and the end.

CrossQuote

Seeking after Christ's kingdom puts everything else in context.

As you think about the CrossQuote, where would you rate its importance in your present life? Being as honest as you can, make a mark on the line to indicate whether you see it as important or insignificant for your daily life.

(Important)   (Insignificant)

Now, go back and look at the CrossQuote again. What do you think you can do to implement this CrossQuote in your life? Jot down a thought or two in the space provided.

Seeking God is backed by a promise!

"Then you will call upon me and come and pray to me, and I will listen to you. You will seek me and find me when you seek me with all your heart" (Jer. 29:12-13).

God's word came to the Hebrews in a despairing time of exile. God reassured them that regardless of their circumstances, He was a God who was with them. He desired to know them intimately and completely. His promise was conditioned upon unreserved, focused seeking on this part. Have you seen this same type of seeking for God from others on your campus? (Check one.)

❏ Yes   ❏ No   ❏ Maybe   ❏ Not sure

The sequence of words 'then/when' implies transformation. Seeking and finding a relationship with God will radically change your priorities and behaviors. This process is grounded in relationship with God, nothing more and nothing less. There are no shortcuts to finding God: not being moral, not going to church, *NOTHING takes the place of experiencing an in-your-face relationship with Jesus Christ.*

CrossQuote

Nothing takes the place of an in-your-face relationship with Jesus Christ.

Why do you suppose it is so important for Christians to have an "in-your-face relationship with Jesus Christ?" Write down at least two reasons. If you need to, talk with a known Christian on campus and get their opinion to this question.

1._____

2._____

3._____

Evan, a student at Virginia Tech University, describes it this way:
"When I feel as if there is nothing left to strive for, I long to see that one pure dream still alive. That is what CrossSeekers does for me. It gives me a source of strength from which to pull. It gives me a goal to shoot for. It doesn't replace my Savior, it helps me know Him better."

So what?

If you were to ask a friend on campus to write an essay about who they see you to be, what would they say is the driving passion in your life? (Jot down some likely answers they might give in the space provided.)

_____

_____

Would they describe you as a seeker of the cross? (Check the one which most applies to how you see yourself spiritually.)
❏ Yes ❏ No ❏ Sometimes

Imagine that you lost your car keys. Chances are you wouldn't just forget about it; you would look everywhere. Your total focus would be finding your keys. As long as they were lost, it would nag your mind. You would probably involve other people in your search. It would consume you until you found them.

In order to find, you must seek. If you lose your keys, you won't find them unless you look for them. It won't happen by osmosis. If you want more from your relationship with Christ, you must seek it. It's that simple.

"You will seek me and find me when you seek me with all your heart" (Jer. 29:13).

What are you earnestly seeking?

Remember Tara and Shawn? They are earnestly seeking their goals by pouring their energies into whatever it takes to reach their dreams. *However, their goals are truly meaningless, unless transformed by Jesus Christ.* Only when their goals become tools for service to Christ will they find life that has eternal value.

Because of God's grace, if you seek, you will find a profoundly intimate relationship with a loving Savior. As a CrossSeeker, you join a group of believers who earnestly seek to know Christ.

Seek and find. Know and grow.

If the CrossQuote is true for your life, list how you feel your life is different because of the CrossQuote in the space provided below. (If you are in a CrossSeekers group, share your answers with another member of your group.)

CrossQuote
Our lifegoals are meaningless unless transformed by Christ.

Nonchalant Christianity

Nonchalant is one of those words that sounds like it is. Nonchalance is apathy. It is a casual "maybe-I-will, maybe-I-won't attitude." How would you define it? Talk with some other students and see if you can come up with at least one other definition of nonchalance. Write that definition here.

Being a CrossSeeker means that you throw off your nonchalant, trite frame of mind. Your life has profound intentionality because Christ has infused meaning into it.

Jesus Christ is relevant and authentic on campus, so we must be relevant and authentic as we seek Him in our lives! In the Bible, we find these words of encouragement:

"Be imitators of God, therefore, as dearly loved children and live a life of love, just as Christ loved us and gave himself up for us as a fragrant offering and sacrifice to God" (Eph. 5:1-2).

Look at the quote from the CrossSeekers Covenant below and **circle your reaction** from the options given following the quote.

As a seeker of the cross of Christ, I am called to break away from trite, nonchalant, laissez-faire Christian living.

Wow!
Not important for me as I live my life on campus.
I can make it authentic in my life.
My roommate wouldn't understand.
I'm confused.
It's worth my commitment.
I think I understand, but I want to know more before I commit.

It's not about nothing!

Students on the campus hunger for relevancy. Relevancy is contrary to randomness, unlike Seinfeld's television show about nothing!

When something is relevant, it is pertinent, fitting, or appropriate. You will find relevancy in Christ because of His sacrificial, fragrant offering. Christ's relevancy comes because He lived an authentic life. And, through His life, He transformed every person He encountered. It's not about nothing, it's about love. Is the "fragrant offering, sacrificial love" of Christ a part of your life?

His kind of love is sacrificial, one that seeks the best for others. It's God—love in action!

CrossQuote
Live a life of Christlike love.

Just as Christ was, CrossSeekers are other-directed, wanting the best spiritually for every other student. Regardless of who you are seen to be on campus by others, you can be "the fragrance of Christ's love."

The Bible tells us in the passage you read earlier that Paul knew to be a follower of Christ, you have to be an imitator of Christ. List some ways you feel Christians on your campus can demonstrate a life of Christlike love to others.

1. _____   2. _____
3. _____   4. _____

The genuine article

Students on the campus hunger for authenticity, for the real thing! Have you ever wondered why advertisements focus on building a brand name? How many students do you know who are drawn to labels because they know that their expectations for value are met? This article is the "real thing."

Christ is no fake. Who you see is Who you get. When you find Christ, you have found the real thing! God valued you so much that He gave up something of infinite value—His Son, Jesus Christ. Not only are expectations for value met in this relationship, but you discover Christ adds value to your life.

Examine the CrossQuote again! Has this been your guiding force in choosing a major? What about your choice of friends on campus? How has this impacted your studies? Has it impacted many of the choices you make every day? Needless to say, these are just questions for thought related to the CrossQuote!

CrossQuote
You find who you are in Christ.

Be imitators of God. As a CrossSeeker, you carry Christ's brand name. Like it or not, this is the journey you have chosen. You won't be sorry! Fashion yourself after His pattern of love.

Think about this statement: *"It's not just a heart thing, it's a head thing, too. You decide to do it."* Now, look at the following list and check those which most reflect the lifestyle you want on campus.
- ❏ I want to be relevant to myself and my friends.
- ❏ I want my Christian walk to be authentic.
- ❏ I don't want to be a fake.
- ❏ I want to share love like Christ did.
- ❏ I want to imitate Christ in all I say and do.

Hopefully you are able to check all of the above. If so, you are beginning to understand what CrossSeekers (the movement) is all about. The Bible says it this way:
"Your attitude should be the same as that of Christ Jesus"
(Phil. 2:5).
"But we have the mind of Christ" (1 Cor. 2:16).

As a student, take on the mind of Christ. The Bible says it is possible!

The way you think and respond models Jesus Christ to yourself, your friends, others on campus, your family. . .and the list goes on and on. How is this possible? Not anything you or I can do. Christ has already done it for us through the power of His Holy Spirit. As the Helper, the Holy Spirit quickens our minds to respond to situations with integrity, spiritually growing, witnessing to others, living a life of purity, developing Christlike relationships, and serving other people.

No randomness, no irrelevancy. Life in Christ is packed with meaning.

Remember Tara and Shawn? They would not characterize their lives as nonchalant. They are focused on achieving great things. But something is tragically missing. Their goals are not wrapped up in the meaning of the cross. Their lives are irrelevant.

Until Tara and Shawn acknowledge the Master's plan in their lives, all that they seek will be a shadow of what God desires for them to do and be! Check out these words from the Apostle Paul in a letter he wrote to new Christians in Philippi.

"But whatever was to my profit I now consider loss for the sake of Christ" (Phil. 3:7).

CrossQuote
CrossSeekers are compelled to live for the sake of Christ.

Think about one or more persons you feel are living for Christ. Do you know any? If so, write their first name(s) down on the space below.

_____

Did you make this choice because they are living for the sake of Christ? You can, too!

Live more: Consecrated recklessness for Christ

"I accept the challenge to divine daring, to consecrated recklessness for Christ, to devout adventure in the face of ridiculing contemporaries."

Check out this part of the Covenant statement. Did you really read it? What does it say to you? In a few words, rephrase the Covenant quote above like you were going to share it with someone who doesn't know what being a CrossSeeker is all about.

_____

_____

_____

Read the following passages of scripture:

"Therefore, I urge you, brothers, in view of God's mercy, to offer your bodies as living sacrifices, holy and pleasing to God—this is your spiritual act of worship" (Rom. 12:1).

"I can do everything through him who gives me strength" (Phil. 4:13).

"I pray that out of his glorious riches he may strengthen you with power through his Spirit in your inner being" (Ephesians 3:16).

As these passages sink in and the reality of what they are saying becomes a part of who you are, check one or more of the choices to indicate your feelings right now.

❑ excited	❑ happy	❑ uneasy
❑ afraid	❑ sad	❑ ready to do it
❑ anxious	❑ challenged	❑ powerful
❑ directed	❑ special	❑ can't do it
❑ undecided	❑ other_____	

Take it personally! What can you do this week to demonstrate your faith and strength is in Christ? List two things you can do this week.

1. _____

2. _____

Accept the challenge! God's power cuts to your inner core through the Holy Spirit and will give you the strength and direction and courage you need.

CrossQuote

Go to the edge of your faith, trust in God and do more!

When you commit your loyalty to Christ, your life of love (being focused on others' needs) becomes an act of worship to Him. Your source of strength comes from the Master.

God's power strengthens you so that you may glorify Him.

How good are you at memorizing? As an exercise to implant God's word into your life, see if you can memorize the following Scripture.

"But he said to me, 'My grace is sufficient for you, for my power is made perfect in weakness'" (2 Corinthians 12:9).

Divine Daring

As CrossSeekers, this power of Christ within you enables you to accept the challenge of divine daring. Many think they could never live up to the six biblical principles found in the Covenant. Guess what! That's where the "divine daring" comes in. Note the following Scripture:

"If we live, we live to the Lord; and if we die, we die to the Lord. So, whether we live or die, we belong to the Lord" (Rom. 14:8).

It is divine because the challenge comes from God. So...based on trust, empowered with the Holy Spirit, you can go further. You can do more, dare to be more!

In your journey as a CrossSeeker, you have the freedom to try out your spiritual gifts and discover how God has gifted you for divine daring which leads to service with Him:

"To prepare God's people for works of service, so that the body of Christ may be built up until we all reach unity in the faith and in the knowledge of the Son of God and become mature, attaining to the whole measure of the fullness of Christ" (Eph. 4:12-13).

An end result of God putting His Spirit within you is that you will be equipped, given talents, to do works of service. So teach a Bible study, mentor youth, help out at the crisis pregnancy center, share your faith story with someone, visit the elderly, speak out for those who have no voice. Dare to be more!

Although we know the Scripture is true, still we see Christians who are not involved in divine daring and Christian service. Why? Can you list two reasons why you think it's hard for some Christians to live with a "divine daring?"

1. _____

2. _____

Remember Tara and Shawn? They are truly gifted individuals, but until they realize whose they are, they will not unlock their fullest potential and live a life of divine daring.

What advice would you give Tara and Shawn if they were your friends? How can you go to the edge of your faith and do more? Share some ideas in the space below.

Devout Adventure

Another aspect of the CrossSeekers challenge is to be committed to "devout adventure." Devout adventure is best seen in a life fully living for Christ. Imagine that every day your desire is to be with Christ and do what He wants you to do. In John 10:10 we see that it is Christ's desire that we experience a journey of life filled with adventure.

What robs you of living life to its fullest? What keeps you from knowing how to experience devout adventure? This passage describes the relationship of the shepherd to his sheep. If the sheep are not clear about the Master's voice, they can be deceived and ultimately destroyed by thieves.

When you open the Bible and read about what God is doing for us, what do you hear Him saying to you? Check each you know is part of God's plan for your life.
- ❏ Integrity ❏ Service   ❏ Spiritual Growth
- ❏ Christlike Relationships   ❏ Witness ❏ Purity

"The thief comes only to steal and kill and destroy; I have come that they may have life, and have it to the full."
John 10:10

The contrasting blessing we receive by listening to the Shepherd's voice is abundant life—going beyond what is necessary. God desires to give us more than we ever asked for, because of who He is. We can be people of covenantal living. We can live a life of devout adventure.

"How much more will those who receive God's abundant provision of grace and of the gift of righteousness reign in life through the one man, Jesus Christ" (Rom. 5:17).

The Apostle Paul is talking about righteous reign in life. Do you feel you are on the journey as a CrossSeeker and that you are claiming the righteous reign?
   ❏ Yes   ❏ No   If no, can you identify why not?

_____

_____

As CrossSeekers, listening to the Master enables you to unlock all His blessings. This is maximum living!

CrossQuote

God gives beyond what is necessary. What does He require of you?

Derick, a student at Liberty University, shares about CrossSeekers: "This program gives students someone to stand up for, Jesus Christ. CrossSeekers encourages students to take a vow and stand up on their campuses against the flow of moving away from God to moving toward Him."

What are things you know must change in your life because of God's gift and claim on your life? Think about it. Remember, as a CrossSeeker, you are called to...

Do more.

Excellence as a Disciple of Christ

I acknowledge I am created in the image of God and committed to excellence as a disciple of Jesus Christ.

Christ's call to us as CrossSeekers is for us to be who He created us to be. Talk about divine daring and devout adventure! To be "created in the image of God and committed to excellence as a disciple" opens the door for a new type of living. Think about two or three areas where this reality impacts how you live your life on the campus. Now, because you are a disciple of Christ, you will:

1. _____

2. _____

3. _____

Not only did God create you in His image, He formed you uniquely. You know about fingerprints (no two are alike) and how each cell within the body is created from DNA. Science has verified what Christians have always known. Check out the verses in the boxes on each side.

By creating you, God has placed His stamp of approval on you so that you can discover all that He desires for you to be. When you read these passages in the boxes at each side, what type feelings do they invoke? I feel: (Check all that apply for you at this moment on your journey of faith.)

❏ affirmed	❏ confused	❏ challenged	❏ silly
❏ trusted	❏ enabled	❏ out of my league	
❏ loved	❏ empowered	❏ capable	❏ wow
❏ no way	❏ important	❏ flexible	❏ in God's hands

For you created my inmost being; you knit me together in my mother's womb (Ps. 139:13).

This is not a complete listing of your feelings, for sure. But look at what you checked. Hopefully, you are feeling great about your journey this far. God has formed you for His purposes. Think how this impacts your life as a student! If you are doing this study with a small group, share your feelings with them.

Yet, O Lord, you are our Father. We are the clay, you are the potter; we are all the work of your hand (Is. 64:8).

The call to excellence as a disciple of Christ is a daunting one. It involves humility. Remember whose you are—the Potter's clay. Out of your relationship with Him, you will develop these marks of discipleship:

• **Faith** —*"For everyone born of God overcomes the world. This is the victory that has overcome the world, even our faith"* (I John 5:4).

CrossQuote
CrossSeekers are confident about whose they are and where they are going.

• **Hope**—*"And we rejoice in the hope of the glory of God"* (Rom. 5:2).

• **Love**— *"By this all men will know that you are my disciples, if you love one another"* (John 13:35).

Ultimately, you are challenged in Matthew 28:19 to duplicate yourselves as disciples: "Therefore go and make disciples of all nations."

Jesus knew it was a challenge worth seeking. He committed His life to it. Are you willing to commit your life to it, regardless of profession or life circumstances? ❏ Yes ❏ No ❏ Maybe ❏ Not right now

Check out the following sharing by Evan. "This CrossSeekers idea began to look a lot more like work upon further investigation. However, as I examined the rewards, I soon realized it is something that I have long needed. This CrossSeekers Covenant is more than words on paper, it is a promise etched on my heart. To be a person of true character in all I do is something that is required of me. But the strength of this Covenant comes in numbers. Not only is this promise made before God, my Lord, whom I serve, but also before college students and adults around the country. I can take the stand, alone if necessary, and know that I have the support of hundreds of others doing the same thing."

Be more.

MOVEMENT OR MOMENT? CrossSeekers!

Do you believe that you can change the world? Five students in 1806 believed they could. The complete account of this beginning of student missions is in the book Perspectives on the World Christian Movement, from which the following information is taken.

Out of the faith of five students came the Haystack Prayer Revival, which ultimately resulted in the Student Volunteer Movement, and it is believed that no single factor has had greater influence in the worldwide outreach of the church than the Student Volunteer Movement. Here's the story:

In 1806, Samuel Mills enrolled in Williams College and discovered other devout students were interested in the spiritual welfare of students. Each Wednesday and Sunday afternoon, he joined them to pray. That August while praying, Mills and four others were caught by a thunderstorm and sought refuge in a haystack. Their prayer focus that day was how to stir interest among students about foreign missions.

Mills realized that each of them must be willing to respond to God's call. He dared them, "We can do this if we will." Their resolution challenged others to commit to foreign missions.

"Bowed in prayer, these first American student volunteers for foreign missions willed that God should have their lives for service wherever he needed them, and in that self-dedication really gave birth to the first national student missionary society in America." *(Perspectives on the World Christian Movement,* p. 215)

CrossQuote
Your obedience to Christ will change the shape of God's world.

In September 1808, they formed the Society of the Brethren to give themselves to extend the gospel around the world. Then they petitioned denominational leaders of the General Association of Congregational Churches to form a foreign missions society. In 1812, four years from the Haystack Prayer Revival, the first North American missionary society was formed. Missionary hall-of-famers Adoniram Judson and Luther Rice were among the first to serve.

It began with five students!

Their passion for students and for God's world compelled them to pray. *Their obedience to the cross of Christ led them to change the shape of God's world*. By seizing the moment, these young students submitted themselves to God's Holy Spirit. This moment became a movement!

Carpe Diem! Seize the Day! Accept the challenge to be a CrossSeeker during your college/university experience! Change the world with Christ in you!

What are the elements that transform a moment into a movement?

- Samuel Mills sought God's face and seized an opportunity to fulfill God's intentions through students in his world.

- Peter saw the Holy Spirit descend upon believers and affirmed that the gospel was for Jews and Greeks.

- Mary discovered an empty tomb and ran to tell the disciples.

It's a vision thing. They all saw what was really going on, caught the vision, and kept the vision.

They saw, caught, and kept the vision.

CrossQuote
Every moment has eternal significance.

Transforming a moment into a movement on your campus is living with your fingers on the pulse of God, seeking to know His heart's desire and being obedient to His desire. King David wrote the Book of Psalms in the Old Testament in the Bible. He caught the vision. He felt the desire in his own heart. He said it this way:

> *"As the deer pants for streams of water, so my soul pants for you, O God. My soul thirsts for God, for the living God"* (Ps. 42:1-2).

CrossSeekers understand the reality that transforming a moment into a movement means making the most of every opportunity—*seeing every moment as having eternal significance.* Why? Because of our relationship to Jesus and what He did for mankind on the cross. We desire to understand what He did more fully and to transform our lives from a moment into God's movement. We are CrossSeekers.

> *"Be very careful, then, how you live—not as unwise but as wise, making the most of every opportunity, because the days are evil"* (Eph. 5:15-16).

CROSS
SEEKERS

Share a prayer with God to commend your journey as a CrossSeeker. (The prayer here is for guidance purposes only. Put this prayer in your own words.)

Prayer of Commitment

Jesus, transforming a moment into a movement means seeing what you desire, catching your vision for my life through the CrossSeekers Covenant principles, and following through out of obedience to the cross of Christ. I commit myself now to discovering more about the journey You have for me as a CrossSeeker. Thank You for loving me and giving direction to my life. Amen.

"I press on toward the goal to win the prize for which God has called me heavenward in Christ Jesus" (Phil. 3:14).

CrossSeekers was formed as a response to the acute spiritual needs of students. Humbly, it is grounded in a keen sense that if God desires for it to become a movement, it is only by students' responsiveness to God's grace and power.

Do you believe that God in you can change the world?
See the vision.
Catch the vision.
Keep the vision.

Chapter 2

THE CROSS: THE EXPRESSION OF GOD'S NEW COVENANT

by Henry Blackaby

Introduction

It was the early morning hours of April 15, 1912. Sixteen-year-old Edith Brown was terrified. Her father, the wealthy Thomas William Solomon Brown, was helping Edith and her mother into a lifeboat. He remained aboard the Titanic. Standing beside the Reverend Carter, Thomas Brown looked into the eyes of his wife and daughter and promised, "I'll see you in New York." Edith's last glimpse of her father was as he stood aboard the Titanic, his gold pocket watch dangling from his waistcoat, talking with Reverend Carter. When Edith and her mother arrived in New York, they frantically searched for him without success. Brown had been moving his family to America to begin a hotel business. His plans were buried with him four kilometers below the surface of the Atlantic ocean. Eighty-one years later, a salvage company discovered Brown's pocket watch among the wreckage and returned it to Edith. It remains a symbol of a sincere promise, made, but not kept.

Life involves many promises. Some promises are made and kept. Others are spoken with no intention of fulfillment. Even vows made with the best of intentions sometimes never come to pass. Are you someone who keeps promises? Your life will reveal whether or not you are as good as your word. Every stage in life requires you to make commitments. As a student, you will be responsible to fulfill a syllabus for each of your classes. You will make promises to your dating partners, fiance(e), or spouse. You may take vows for your chosen profession. There will be commitments to your friends, your parents, and your employer. Your faithfulness to your promises is vitally important to the destiny of your life.

If you are a Christian, your life is shaped by the commitments you make to God. God is determined to keep His promises to you, because He relates to His people on the basis of a covenant. He takes the initiative to offer a covenant to people. He sets the terms of each covenant; He determines the rewards for keeping the covenant and the penalty for forsaking it. There is life-changing potential in a covenant with God, though He does not force anyone to enter into one. However, if you want to have a meaningful relationship with God, you will find it in keeping a covenant with Him. If you want to experience God, you must be a covenant keeper.

I. God's Covenants in the Old Testament

In Old Testament history, a covenant was a sacred promise between two parties. There were no courts of law or legal contracts to hold people to their promises, so society developed the most binding form of promise it could devise. This became known as a covenant. It was considered inviolable, because the covenant makers solemnly promised before witnesses to keep their word. More importantly, the covenant-making ceremony was conducted before God. Often the covenant makers would kill an animal and cut it in two. The two parts of the sacrificed animal would be separated, and the covenant makers would pass between the two halves. As each party walked through, he would call upon God to witness his oath and to tear him asunder if he did not keep every word of the covenant. This ritual became known as "cutting a covenant." It was a serious commitment, and any breach of the promise invoked a curse upon the offender.

Noah

The Old Testament records several of God's covenants with His people. One of the better known was His vow to Noah after the great flood (Genesis 9:1-17). God promised Noah and his family that He would never again destroy the earth with a flood. The symbol of this promise is the rainbow. Whenever believers see a rainbow, we are reminded of God's promise. God's covenant involved obligations upon Noah and his descendants as well. They were not to commit murder or to eat meat with the blood still in it, and they were to populate and rule the earth. This covenant, which was initiated by God, resulted in prosperity but held obligations for the people who accepted its conditions.

Abraham

God first dealt with Abraham in terms of a covenant. God promised to bless Abraham and make his name great. He said He would bless anyone who blessed Abraham and curse anyone who cursed him. He also promised to bless all the families of the earth because of Abraham's family. As in Noah's case, there were obligations for Abraham. He was to leave his country and trust God to lead him to a distant land (Genesis 12:1-3). God confirmed His covenant with Abraham through a holy covenant-making ceremony. He instructed Abraham to take a three-year-old heifer, a three-year-old female goat, a three-year-old ram, a turtledove, and a pigeon, cut each of them in two and lay the halves opposite each other. Then:

> "When the sun had set and darkness had fallen, a smoking firepot with a blazing torch appeared and passed between the pieces. On that day the Lord made a covenant with Abram and said, 'To your descendants I give this land, from the river of Egypt to the great river, the Euphrates . . .'" (Genesis 15:17-19).

In that sacred moment, God assured Abraham that He would keep His promise. Whenever circumstances seemed to make God's promise unattainable, Abraham would draw hope from the memory of God's solemn vow. When Abraham was 99 years old, God reaffirmed His covenant:

"I am God Almighty; walk before me and be blameless. I will confirm my covenant between me and you and will greatly increase your numbers." Abram fell facedown, and God said to him, "As for me, this is my covenant with you: You will be the father of many nations. No longer will you be called Abram; your name will be Abraham, for I have made you a father of many nations. I will make you very fruitful; I will make nations of you, and kings will come from you. I will establish my covenant as an everlasting covenant between me and you and your descendants after you for the generations to come, to be your God and the God of your descendants after you. The whole land of Canaan, where you are now an alien, I will give as an everlasting possession to you and your descendants after you; and I will be their God." Then God said to Abraham, "As for you, you must keep my covenant, you and your descendants after you for the generations to come. This is my covenant with you and your descendants after you, the covenant you are to keep: Every male among you shall be circumcised. You are to undergo circumcision, and it will be the sign of the covenant between me and you. For the generations to come every male among you who is eight days old must be circumcised, including those born in your household or bought with money from a foreigner—those who are not your offspring" (Genesis 17:1-12).

Observe the lasting nature of the covenant—it would still apply to people living centuries later. This time, circumcision would be the sign to remind God's people that they belonged to Him and had obligations to Him. God pledged to Abraham that his descendants would inherit the promised land. This was the promise Moses and the children of Israel claimed as they fled from Egypt many hundreds of years later.

Moses
Perhaps the pinnacle of God's covenants with His people in the Old Testament involved Moses and the Law. After freeing the Israelites from Egypt, God led them to Mount Sinai where He gave Moses the Ten Commandments and the rest of the Law. Before entering the promised land, God's people had to pledge to follow His holy standards. God was holy, and He expected His people to live holy lives (Leviticus 11:44). If His people trusted Him and obeyed Him, God would give them victory and prosperity wherever they went. The covenant would be available to each succeeding generation, provided they accept and keep the terms of the covenant. Throughout the rest of the Old Testament, the prophets' condemnations of the Israelites would be for not keeping their commitments to God. Whenever God chastised His people, He did so on the grounds

that they had violated their covenant with Him and thus deserved punishment for breaking their word.

The Ten Commandments and the rest of the Old Testament law became symbolic of God's covenant with His people. God's law was precious to His devout followers, and they made every effort to keep it to the letter. It became apparent, however, that, in spite of great effort, no one could live a perfect life and keep the law exactly. The harder people attempted to keep the law, the more obvious it became that no one could. God gradually revealed through His prophets that apart from divine intervention, every person, regardless of his or her piety, would fall short of God's high standard for His people. God's covenants in the Old Testament anticipated a Savior—Someone who could enable people to properly relate to God. As the centuries passed, God's people waited and longed for the day when His promises would be fulfilled through the Messiah.

Delayed

Jim Post was a door-to-door salesman in Windsor, Ontario during the Depression. Since jobs were scarce and money even scarcer, Jim needed an edge. In 1934, hoping to improve his sales skills, Post ordered a book from the National Salesman Training Association of Chicago. It was shipped out but somehow waylaid, and he never received it. In 1996, letter carrier Beth Bailey noticed an unusual parcel in her delivery bag. When she examined the date stamped on the faded yellow paper, she was amazed. It had been processed for delivery 62 years earlier! She discovered Post no longer lived at the address on the package. Bailey began asking people in Post's old neighborhood if they knew where he had gone. Finally, a long-time resident suggested Bailey check a nearby senior citizen's home. Sure enough, he was there and quite bewildered to receive a book on sales techniques. He certainly didn't need it now that he was 105 years old!

God's timing is perfect. We are so enslaved by time we often forget that God sees things from the perspective of eternity. At times we may feel He's forgotten us or changed His mind, yet nothing can thwart God's promises. Nothing can rush them into fulfillment before their proper time. The promises God made in the Old Testament took centuries to come to pass, but when the time was right, Jesus fulfilled every promise His Father had made.

II. God's Covenant in the New Testament

God's conclusive solution for mankind's sin was His Son Jesus. Jesus lived a perfect life on our behalf. He alone paid the penalty for our unrighteous living. Scripture records that although He knew the cross awaited Him, *"Jesus resolutely set out for Jerusalem" (Luke 9:51)*. As the horror of crucifixion loomed before Him, Jesus acknowledged *"it was for this very reason I came to this hour" (John 12:27)*.

How similar the sacrifices of the Old Testament and the New Testament—and yet how infinitely more precious was the sacrifice of God's own Son! To symbolize the sacred nature of a covenant in Old Testament times, an innocent animal would shed its blood. The new covenant would be sealed by the blood of God's blameless only Son. At the Last Supper with His disciples, Jesus said, *"Drink from it, all of you. This is my blood of the covenant, which is poured out for many for the forgiveness of sins" (Matthew 26:27-28)*.

The new covenant would supersede God's old covenant. This one would not be symbolized by circumcision or by the law; the enduring symbol of the new covenant would be the cross. The cross represents God's definitive answer to man's sin.

Suffering

Leslie Szabo wanted to become a mother, but she did not want to endure any pain in the process. According to a newspaper account in the *Calgary Herald,* the 44-year-old chartered accountant was expecting twins. Claiming she was extremely sensitive to pain, Szabo demanded that the Hamilton Health Sciences Corporation guarantee her a painless delivery. They promised they would do everything possible to keep her reasonably free from pain during the delivery. She was greatly disappointed. She claimed that she suffered "traumatic" and "unnecessary" distress giving birth. In court she argued that the debilitating pain and trauma had prevented her from being a good mother, eroded her enjoyment of life, and caused her to lose her $100,000 a year job. So she launched a $2.4 million lawsuit against the medical center. The court did not find in her favor and ordered her to pay the legal expenses of those she had accused.

Szabo's case made headlines. The court declared that there is no painless way to give birth. Scripture agrees with the court's decision. Giving birth has always involved pain (Genesis 3:16). God our Father wanted to give us new life. The price was horrific, the pain enormous. The cross is a graphic symbol that Christ willingly suffered great anguish to make spiritual rebirth available to everyone who would accept His gift.

One cannot understand Christ apart from an examination of the cross. The cross is like a prism; there are many facets, each one providing a slightly different view of God's character. Thus, a study of the cross is actually many studies, each one revealing a profound truth about the Lord.

The Meaning of the Cross

1. God's Love

The cross is a well-known emblem today for believers and non-believers alike. Often people wear a cross as a piece of jewelry. Today the cross engenders good feelings for many who see it. But this was not so in Jesus' day. Then, the cross was the most painful and humiliating death known to man. The cross fostered fear and revulsion in those who saw it. Only deep, divine love could motivate Jesus to suffer the cross so that even those who mocked Him could be spared. Scripture indicates *"God so loved the world that He gave His one and only Son, that whoever believes in Him shall not perish but have eternal life" (John 3:16)*. We need never doubt God's love—the cross is unquestionable proof of how much He cares for us. The Apostle John observed:

> *"This is how we know what love is: Jesus Christ laid down his life for us. . . This is how God showed his love among us: He sent his one and only Son into the world that we might live through him. This is love: not that we loved God, but that he loved us and sent his Son as an atoning sacrifice. . ." (1 John 3:16, 4:9-10).*

On the cross, Jesus forever proved that God loves us. The cross is our assurance that, having gone to such immeasurable lengths to save us, He will never allow anything to separate us from His love (Romans 8:37-39).

2. God's Mercy

God's new covenant, as signified by the cross, also shows His mercy. God's righteousness demanded that sin be punished and His holiness upheld. God demonstrated mercy by withholding the punishment we deserved. The evidence of God's mercy is the cross. Sin has been paid for on the cross, freeing every sinner to ask for mercy in the name of Jesus Christ. No sin is great enough to exhaust the unfathomable mercy of God (1 John 1:9).

3. God's Grace

The cross represents God's unfathomable grace given freely to us, though we are undeserving. Through the cross of Jesus, God graciously offers eternal life to repentant sinners (Ephesians 2:8-9). Everyone who accepts this gift becomes a child of God through spiritual birth (John 1:12-13). As God's children, we also become *"heirs, and joint heirs with Christ" (Romans 8:16-17)*. We have *"everything we need for life and godliness" (2 Peter 1:3)*. Like mercy, grace is an undeserved gift. The cross perfectly symbolizes the grace relationship we enjoy with our Creator.

4. The Gravity of Sin

Sin is so deplorable to the Father that He could not look the other way, though the solution meant an excruciating death for His Son. The drastic cost of crucifixion is clear evidence of sin's repugnance to God. Sin was destroying His creation; therefore, at the cross, God *"made him who had no sin to be sin for us, so that in him we might become the righteousness of God" (2 Corinthians 5:21).* Even the humiliation of the cross did not deter God from providing a Savior so we could have life. Do you ever wonder how God views your sin? Look closely at the cross.

5. God's Holiness

God is holy; there can be no fellowship with Him—no access to Him— without holiness. God expects holiness to permeate every part of our lives (1 Peter 1:16). Yet how are we, who are imperfect, to attain holiness? The Law that God gave in the Old Testament pointed the way to holiness but did not provide the means to achieve it. Only the cross, and the relationship with God that the cross makes possible, can make a sinful person holy.

6. Eternity

One of the most difficult things for mortal humanity to grasp is the truth of eternity. Until we begin to understand the magnitude of the eternal consequences surrounding the cross, we'll never comprehend all that was at stake. God, *"not wanting anyone to perish, but everyone to come to repentance" (2 Peter 3:9),* sent His Son to the cross to provide eternal life to all who would accept it. Whether we realize it or not, we were created for eternity. Therefore, God does not relate to us as strictly finite creatures. The cross forever settled eternity for those who accept God's salvation and for those who reject it.

7. The Heart of Christ

The cross gives us a dramatic look at the heart of Christ. There we see His intense devotion to His Father. Jesus said:
"When you have lifted up the Son of Man, then you will know that I am the one I claim to be, and that I do nothing on my own but speak just what the Father has taught me. The one who sent me is with me; he has not left me alone, for I always do what pleases Him" (John 8:28-29).

Jesus' attitude of absolute obedience to His Father was clearly seen at His crucifixion. Obedience to His Father was life itself to Jesus. He said, *"My food. . .is to do the will of him who sent me and to finish his work" (John 4:34).* (See also John 5:30 and 6:38.) He was so totally committed to His Father that He remained undaunted even as He faced a torturous death on a cross.

The cross is not only a testimony of the Savior's devotion and obedience to His Father, it also demonstrates Christ's incredible love for us. The apostle Paul wrote:

"Grace and peace to you from God our Father and the Lord Jesus Christ, who gave himself for our sins to rescue us from the present evil age, according to the will of our God and Father . . ." (Galatians 1:3-4). (See also Romans 5:14-15, Galatians 2:20, Revelation 1:5.)

8. God's Power

The cross is spectacular proof of God's awesome power. Evil men did everything they could to destroy Jesus. Satan and his forces of darkness marshaled all their powers to kill Jesus. Death, mankind's greatest enemy, desperately held Jesus in its vice grip. But the Lord was triumphant! NOTHING could prevent the Father from raising His Son on the third day! The cross and the empty tomb that followed proves that nothing can prevent God from carrying out His plans. This is true for our lives as well (1 Corinthians 1:18).

Conclusion

The cross of Christ is the symbol of God's new covenant with His people. As such, it is at the very heart of the Christian's life. Studying the cross, learning the truths it teaches about God, and responding in obedience will prepare you to be a CrossSeeker.

III. Implications of the New Covenant

The cross clearly reveals what God has offered through the new covenant—love, mercy, grace, holiness, victory over sin, and eternal life with Him. As in all of God's covenants, there are obligations for both partners. As you join in a covenant with God, your obligation is to become a CrossSeeker and to model your life after the example of Christ.

1. A CrossSeeker's Heart

Jesus offered the new covenant to His disciples with these conditions: "If anyone would come after me, he must deny himself and take up his cross and follow me" (Matthew 16:24). Taking up your cross is a choice. The new covenant is available only to those who embrace Christ's saving work on the cross, willingly joining Him by following His example. In other words, a CrossSeeker is one whose heart is like the Savior's heart.

Certainly, such a heart does not come naturally. Apart from God's work in our lives, we are just as incapable of fulfilling the new covenant as Old Testament people were of fulfilling the old covenant. The good news is that along with eternal salvation, the new covenant also brings a radical heart-transformation in every believer. Paul explained it this way: *"I have been crucified with Christ and I no longer live, but Christ lives in me. The life I live in the body, I live by faith in the Son of God, who loved me and gave himself for me" (Galatians 2:20)*. Paul had been a proud, self-righteous Pharisee before he met Christ. Then he experienced salvation and his life was so changed he called himself a *"servant"* and *"prisoner of Jesus Christ" (Romans 1:1, Philemon 1:1)*. The cross captivated Paul. His heart was transformed. Now, for the first time, he was capable of fulfilling the requirements of God's covenant. The moment Paul became a Christian, the Holy Spirit entered him and began to change every area of his life. Paul was adamant that to experience the full impact of this transformation, you must *"work out your salvation with fear and trembling, for it is God who works in you to will and to act according to his good purpose" (Philippians 2:12-13)*. The new covenant is unique in that God not only sets a standard for His people, He also enables us to meet the standard through His Holy Spirit.

2. A CrossSeeker's Attitude

A CrossSeeker's attitude is to do the Father's will just as our Savior, Jesus Christ, did. God chooses to accomplish His purposes through those *"whose hearts are fully committed to him" (2 Chronicles 16:9)*. As we stand humbly before the cross and submit our lives to the Father, He will involve us in His mission to save those who are spiritually lost. Once again, our model is our Savior: *"Although he was a son, he learned obedience from what he suffered [the cross] and, once made perfect, he became the source of eternal salvation for all who obey him" (Hebrews 5:8-9)*. A CrossSeeker's attitude, therefore, is one of obedience.

3. A CrossSeeker's Witness

Jesus said:

> "I tell you the truth, unless a kernel of wheat falls to the ground and dies, it remains only a single seed. But if it dies, it produces many seeds. The man who loves his life will lose it, while the man who hates his life in this world will keep it for eternal life. Whoever serves me must follow me; and where I am, my servant also will be. My Father will honor the one who serves me" (John 12:24-26).

Jesus gave up *everything* in exchange for a cross, so we could possess everything. Jesus became poor for us so we, through His poverty, might become rich (2 Corinthians 8:9). He bore in His body our sin and pain so we could be free (Isaiah 53:4-5). He provided a way for us because we had lost our way (Isaiah 53:6). He did all of this when He willingly gave His life on the cross.

If you are a Christian, all that you have as a new creation was bought for you on the cross. Through the cross, you have received forgiveness for your sins. Christ's sacrifice has purchased your peace with the Father. When you accepted God's gift, you became His heir and you now have the resources of heaven at your disposal. You will enjoy an eternal destiny spent in the presence of Almighty God. All of this and much more is yours as a result of your response to the cross. Your life, therefore, ought to be a testimony to the life-transforming work of the cross. Paul explained it this way: *"For we are to God the aroma of Christ among those who are being saved and those who are perishing. To the one we are the smell of death; to the other, the fragrance of life" (2 Corinthians 2:15-16).* As a CrossSeeker, you should be a living example of God's merciful love, His astonishing grace, and His matchless power.

Summary

When we accept the new covenant offered to us through Jesus Christ, we inherit all the promises and blessings God has pledged to those who receive Christ. We also commit ourselves to live according to the holy standard God requires in Scripture. We give up the freedom to choose how and when we will live *for* Christ and we endeavor instead to be *like* Christ. A covenant with God affects every area of our lives; it involves changes, sometimes difficult changes. When we choose to become CrossSeekers, we are making a total, life-long commitment to know and experience Christ and to emulate Him as the Holy Spirit empowers us.

When we accept God's invitation to become CrossSeekers, we are also agreeing to:
- maintain *integrity*
- pursue *spiritual growth*
- *witness* to others about what God has done in our lives
- *serve* others
- pursue *purity*
- seek only *Christlike relationships* in every area of our lives

Challenge

I vividly recall an encounter I had with God when I was a young man. One day God got my attention and spoke to my heart in a way I will never forget. He gave me a deep concern for my country and for the countless people who did not know Christ. He put a burden on my heart for the many towns and cities that had no church. I sensed God saying to me,

"Henry, I could use your life to make a difference in this needy world." Then God laid before me the conditions. He made me keenly aware of the importance for my life to be holy. He reminded me of the need to spend regular time with Him so I would know His heart and understand His will. That day I pledged to the Lord with all my heart that I would strive to be holy and to know and walk with Him. From that day onward I began to see God bring me opportunities to serve Him in ways I never anticipated. God developed my character and revealed His power and His love to me in dimensions which I had never dreamed. He has been absolutely faithful to keep His promises. In fact, He has blessed my life and used my life to bless others far more than I could have ever expected. Whenever the covenant has been broken, it has not been God's fault, but mine. I have not always been faithful to keep my commitments to Him. At times I have allowed sin to creep into my life. I have sometimes neglected my time *with* Him in my effort to work *for* Him. My failure to keep my commitment to God has cost me, and others around me, God's blessings. But every time I have repented and returned to my relationship with Him, He has been faithful to forgive me and to continue working in my life as He promised. I am an ordinary person who has been in covenant with an extraordinary God!

God has wonderful blessings in store for you as well. He has promised in His Word to provide for you everything that comes with being a child of God and to use your life for His glory. He stands ready to keep His promises to you. Are you willing to take God at His word and respond with equal commitment to His invitation? I pray you will be a CrossSeeker.

Chapter 3

THE CROSS:
EXPOSING CONTEMPORARY
COMMITMENTS

A Promise Made

I was a second-year college student, and I was broke. I had no idea how to raise enough money to pay for tuition in January. A friend suggested working at a remote logging camp 18 hours away over Christmas break. It sounded great—a fast way to make good money. I started making plans. Everything went like clockwork until I informed my mother of my pending departure.

"You will be home by Christmas, won't you?" she asked. I was her oldest child, and we realized there might not be many more Christmases together. Hastily, I promised I would. At the time, the promise seemed like an easy one to keep. I would work until Christmas Eve, then journey home.

Life has a way of foiling best-laid plans. As soon as I arrived, the logging outfit experienced mechanical difficulties, delaying operations. No work, no pay. Christmas approached, and I realized I had earned a fraction of the money I needed. My boss urged me to stay over Christmas to make the "big money" now that the machinery was repaired. My parents could not afford to help with my tuition, so I was sorely tempted. As I considered my dilemma, I heard the weather forecast for Christmas Eve—minus forty degrees and a blizzard.

My mother would not want me to travel on hazardous roads. Yet I could still hear my casual promise, assuring her that she could count on me to be home by Christmas. I felt that I should keep my promise, so . . . I set out for home. It was the most treacherous, prayer-filled trip I had ever made. Traffic was congested along the highway. Ice formed on my car's windshield wipers. Numerous vehicles littered the snowy ditches. Mile after mile, there was just enough open road to keep plodding my way home. I finally pulled into our driveway. The rest of my family had gone to a Christmas Eve service. My mother stayed behind, watching the clock, worried about my safety. She knew if it were possible, I would come. I'll never forget the look on her face as I wearily trudged into the house. She met me with a huge smile and a warm embrace, and I knew my effort to keep my word had been worth it.

Sometimes the commitments we make become harder to keep than we first imagined. Promises made in haste can come back to haunt us when we realize the price we have to pay to keep them. The world's approach to keeping commitments is radically different from God's commitment to His promises. Our complex society presents innumerable obstacles which challenge

Sometimes the commitments we make become harder to keep than we first imagined.

our commitments. Society often treats commitments as holding no binding effect upon the promise-maker. The consequences for breaking commitments are minimized or excused.

Focus on the Cross

The cross is the constant focus of the CrossSeeker's life. It is the standard by which we measure our lives. The apostle Paul claimed: "For I resolved to know nothing while I was with you except Jesus Christ and him crucified" (1 Corinthians 2:2). Paul understood that the cross of Jesus Christ was central to the Christian's life. The cross illuminates every aspect of our lives. We must evaluate our actions in light of its standard.

Shedding Light on a Masterpiece

Today's technology is shedding new light on the world's treasures. Leonardo da Vinci's masterpiece, the Mona Lisa, came under intense scrutiny with the advent of computers. Modern technology revealed that someone changed what da Vinci had originally painted. A mountain range in the background and Mona Lisa's necklace in the original painting were painted over. To the naked eye these modifications were indiscernible. To the probing analysis of high-tech computers, every mistake and cover-up became obvious.

Jesus' death on the cross exposes every sin and shortcoming in our lives. Nothing escapes the penetrating light of the cross. It remains the perfect standard against which everything is measured. We may attempt to present our lives as "masterpieces" of faithfulness, but the cross penetrates beyond any facade. This is true for the commitments we make. They must be measured against God's standard found in scripture.

List two areas of your life you need to evaluate in light of the standard of the cross. (Remember, this is your book, and no one should see your answers unless you give permission.)

1. _____

2. _____

God's Commitment: The Cross

The greatest commitment ever made was God's commitment to the cross. His plan to save sinful humanity required the death of His only Son. The road to the cross was filled with obstacles and opposition. The powers of darkness battled against Jesus. The religious establishment persecuted Him. His friends deserted Him; one betrayed Him. But having resolved to bring salvation to mankind, God remained undeterred.

The Genesis Promise

The Bible records many promises made by God. God approached Abram with a promise to create a special group of people through whom He would send a Savior:

". . . you will be a blessing.
I will bless those who bless you,
and whoever curses you I will curse;
and all peoples on earth will be blessed through you" (Genesis 12:2-3).

God's answer for man's sin came in His promise that He would bless Abram and his descendants. Abram's descendants would have the unique opportunity to bring people into a special relationship with God; thus Abraham's descendants would provide a blessing to the entire world.

The Promise in Psalms

God later clarified His promise. One of Abram's descendants would suffer on behalf of all people. The Psalmist described what the promised Savior would endure:

"My God, my God, why have you forsaken me? . . . All who see me mock me; they hurl insults, shaking their heads: 'He trusts in the Lord; let the Lord rescue him.' I am poured out like water, and all my bones are out of joint. My heart has turned to wax; . . .a band of evil men has encircled me, they have pierced my hands and my feet. . . They divide my garments among them and cast lots for my clothing" (Psalm 22:1, 7-8, 14, 16, 18).

This graphic passage elaborates on God's promise. Abraham's descendant would purchase salvation for humanity, but the cost would be great.

God's Promise by the Prophet

Hundreds of years after the Psalmist wrote, God further revealed His covenant through the prophet Isaiah. He painted a dramatic picture of the Savior's suffering:

"He was despised and rejected by men, a man of sorrows, and familiar with suffering. Like one from whom men hide their faces he was despised, and we esteemed him not. Surely he took up our infirmities and carried our sorrows, yet we considered him stricken by God, smitten by him, and afflicted. But he was pierced for our transgressions, he was crushed for our iniquities; the punishment

*that brought us peace was upon him, and by his wounds we are
healed. . . He was oppressed and afflicted, yet he did not open his
mouth; he was led like a lamb to the slaughter, and as a sheep
before her shearers is silent, so he did not open his mouth. By
oppression and judgment he was taken away. . . For he was cut off
from the land of the living; for the transgression of my people he
was stricken. . . Yet it was the Lord's will to crush him and cause
him to suffer . . ." (Isaiah 53:3-5, 7-8, 10).*

Even the horror of the cross could not deter the Father from His commitment to present His beloved Son as a sacrifice for our sin.

God's promise neared its fulfillment as Jesus was born and lived out His
sinless life. During Jesus' last days, it must have grieved the Father to
watch as Jesus' disciple betrayed Him and His friend denied Him. God
must have agonized to watch the callous Roman soldiers torture and mock
His Son. How heartbreaking to hear the deafening shouts of, "Crucify
Him," from the lips of the very ones for whom Jesus was suffering. How
painful to release His Son's fate to an unscrupulous Roman politician more
concerned with political victories than justice. How torturous to witness
the brutal Roman soldiers viciously drive clumsy spikes through His Son's
hands and feet, when God knew that He could release His Son at any
moment. How difficult it must have been to hear His Son pray, "Father
take this cup from me," and yet to know that He could not save His Son
and save mankind. Yet, because God was faithful to His promise, Jesus
could ultimately cry out in triumph, "It is finished" (John 19:30).

The Bible is extremely clear on this point—God keeps His promises!
*"What I have said, that will I bring about; what I have planned,
that will I do" (Isaiah 46:11).*

The cross testifies that God would go to great lengths to fulfill His
commitment. Nothing could hinder God's faithfulness to His word. No
resistance could discourage Him, no betrayal could devastate Him. No
ungratefulness could dishearten Him.

God, as Creator, sets our standard. He takes His commitments seriously.
We can do no less.

Review the scripture you just read once again. Think about God's example of faithfulness—sending His sinless Son to die a cruel death for your sins. Once you have done this, what emotion describes your reaction? (Check all that apply.)

❑ shock   ❑ disbelief   ❑ wonder   ❑ don't care   ❑ excited
❑ not sure ❑ glad to be a CrossSeeker   ❑ bewildered
❑ don't understand   ❑ grateful   ❑ believe

FOCUS ON TODAY'S COMMITMENTS

1. Commitments to Parents

For generations, youth generally adopted their parents' values, customs, and religion. The social revolution of the 1960s radically changed the way we view our parents. Suddenly, the younger generation assumes their adults are out of touch with reality. The values of anyone over 40 are flatly rejected. With the advances in retirement benefits and specialized homes for the elderly, people no longer assume the obligation to care for elderly or sick relatives. This becomes the responsibility of the government and insurance companies. *Respecting one's parents is restrictive and cast off, condemned as old-fashioned.*

Respecting one's parents is restrictive and cast off, condemned as old-fashioned.

Entering college, new situations force you to examine commitments to your family. Perhaps you were raised in a Christian home where godly morals were taught. This may be the first time in your life to decide which church to attend, or whether to attend at all. Moral standards taken for granted when you lived at home may be ridiculed on campus. Christian beliefs, assumed true in your home, may be mocked by your professors and fellow students. Even if you did not grow up in a Christian home, you must decide whether to adopt or discard the attitudes, values, and lifestyles that you learned as a child.

As you grow increasingly independent of your parents, you must consider your obligations to them. Do you return home for holiday gatherings or when they are sick? What are your commitments if your parents divorce? If your parents disagree with your choices or become angry with you, do you have an obligation to be reconciled with them?

Jot down two reasons students may consider respecting their parents is "old-fashioned" today:

1. _____

2. _____

2. Commitments to Boyfriends and Girlfriends

Students with no hope for eternity want to enjoy life on earth to the fullest. Long-term relationships are too demanding when one lives for the moment. Many students will forego marriage vows because, although they feel they love their partner today, there is no guarantee of loving them tomorrow. College couples who are dating readily have sex without considering the ramifications for the future. You may know students on the campus with this mindset. Often, even basic commitments such as honesty and respect in relationships are ignored. Date rape, unwanted pregnancies, and sexually transmitted diseases are some results of student's unwillingness to commit themselves fully to each other. Many students confuse commitment with feelings, reasoning that when feelings are gone, the obligation to love someone vanishes as well.

In The News: A Serial Groom

A classic case of a shallow, selfish view of relationships is the story of Glynn "Scotty" Wolf. According to a newspaper account, Wolf hated to be alone and wanted constant companionship. To that end, he married—29 times. Although Wolf repeatedly promised before God and witnesses to love each spouse "so long as we both shall live," he discarded every one of them, some after only a few days. Tragically, for a man who had taken 29 wives and produced 40 children during his 89 years, only one child, and none of his former wives attended his funeral. He was destitute and alone when he died. No one was willing to claim his body or to pay for his funeral. One of the few possessions remaining at his death was a wedding dress hanging in his closet, "just in case." Wolf selfishly sought others to meet his needs, yet he felt no obligation to follow through on the vows he made so casually.

What causes people to treat people like that?

3. Commitment to Friends

The world you live in is confused about what friendship is. Biblically, a friend in the true sense is someone who "loves at all times" (Proverbs 17:17). In our sinfulness, we have abused the privilege of friendship. I may have a friend today, but if I become interested in his girlfriend, or if my life becomes too busy, or if he begins to have too many needs, I can discard him. *Friendships are often focused on what we can get, rather than on what we can give.* The earth

Friendships are often focused on what we can get, rather than on what we can give.

grows more populous, yet there have never been more lonely people. Students go to great lengths to break their loneliness. Some join cults, others compromise their values and become involved in crime, drugs, or promiscuity, all in the effort to find love and acceptance.

Friendships these days are tenuous. The transitory nature of our lives and increasing demands on our time make long-term friendships hard to maintain. It takes a lot of effort to nurture a close friendship, and the challenges involved mean fewer people are willing to pay the price.

Friends Until Death

Two eighteen-year-olds from Iowa were best friends. They did everything together. Then, tragically, as reported to the Calgary Herald, they both became depressed and anxious about the future. Neither was able to help the other find answers to their seemingly insurmountable problems. They lost hope. As they spiraled down into an emotional pit of despair, they adopted a grim plan. They left suicide notes for their parents, stole a car, and fled toward Niagara Falls. They robbed and killed a store owner, then entered Canada. Canadian police disabled their car and began closing in on them. In a final desperate act, the two friends, realizing capture was imminent, pointed guns at each other and simultaneously pulled the triggers. Sadly, rather than helping one another, these friends merely accelerated each other's rush to destruction.

4. Job Commitment

In the 1950s most college graduates found a job, took out a long-term mortgage, and settled in to work for the same company until retirement. Today, such loyalty on the part of both employee and employer no longer exists. Corporate takeovers, gigantic shifts in the global economy, technological advances, and burgeoning personnel costs resulted in job security becoming obsolete. Likewise, an expanded marketplace coupled with a dizzying array of courses and seminars for upgrading skills has provided employees with far more options for employment than ever before. The result? Few people retire with the same company they start with. More significantly, *fewer employees sense an obligation to act with integrity as they work for their present employer*, since they suspect that their employer is not committed to them, and they know they will probably leave for a better job anyway.

> Fewer employees sense an obligation to act with integrity as they work for their present employer...

There is nothing wrong with moving to a better job, but sadly, with the transitory nature of the workforce has also come a loose value system of what is now ethical in the workplace. The media is filled with stories of employees who embezzled and stole property from their company. The prevailing attitude is: "It's only wrong if you get caught!" Work ethics have steadily deteriorated to the point that a hard-working employee can actually be ostracized by his colleagues for making them look bad by comparison.

Could this be true of a good "student" as well? (Check one.)
❑ Yes   ❑ No   ❑ Sometimes

Dishonesty in the Office

David Shum worked for TDA Management Inc. He was responsible for managing the investments of 79-year-old Olga Monkman. Shum won her complete trust and then systematically embezzled $135,230 from her account, as told in a local newspaper. That his victim was an elderly widow seemed to have no effect on his conscience. When Shum was discovered, he lied to Mrs. Monkman, telling her his daughter had a rare blood disease, and he had desperately needed the money.

5. Commitment to Churches

Reginald Bibby, a Canadian sociologist, says in the book Fragmented Gods, that people in North America prefer "religion `a la carte." That is, they look at churches as one large ecclesiastical buffet where they are free to select items which appeal to their appetites and to bypass things they find unattractive. The fundamental question for many is not, "Where can I make the greatest contribution?" but, "What church will provide the most for me?" If Church A has more activities for college students than Church B, then I will attend Church A. That does not, however, prevent me from skipping a service at Church A if Church C has a special speaker or if Church D has a famous singer on a particular Sunday. I may also switch to Church E if several of my friends decide to attend there.

6. Commitment to Ethical Standards

In times past, certain ethical standards were assumed to be firmly believed and observed by society. "Honesty is the best policy" was an accepted truism. Hard work, caring for your family, and loyalty were values commonly held. Professions such as medicine, law, and education had codes of ethics which were generally considered to be inviolable. However, today's newspapers regularly herald ethical violations by those society used to trust. Religious and political leaders are routinely exposed as immoral and dishonest. Teachers are caught sexually abusing their students. Doctors are charged with malpractice. Lawyers steal from their clients. The list could go on and on.

Check your local newspaper! Write down one example you can find where a commitment to ethical standards no longer seems to exist.

7. Cheating on the Increase

Although the majority still affirm that "honesty is the best policy," a growing percentage of people admit they will cheat if they think they can get away with it. A poll by a prominent magazine indicated that 24% of respondents admitted they would not correct a waitress if she undercharged them for a meal, 9% would keep a wallet filled with cash if they found it, one-third would cheat on their income tax, and almost 25% would steal 10 million dollars if they knew they would not get caught.

In colleges, the incidences of cheating are increasing, especially with the popularity of the Internet. In my research, I discovered Kenny Sahr, who introduced a website in 1996 entitled: "School Sucks," in which over 2,500 essays were available for purchase to inquirers. (This chapter is not one of them.) Numerous services are now available to the dishonest student. A "Write My Essay" Internet service welcomes you to its site this way: "Thank you for choosing writemyessay.com. At writemyessay.com, we are confident that you will receive the highest quality custom paper available anywhere. Our expert writers are all college graduates and all have an emphasis in writing." The charge is $20 for the first page and $10 for each additional page. They accept major credit cards. Various studies of university students have found from 75% to 90% of students polled admitted to cheating. One student in a science class did not answer any of the multiple choice questions and kept the blank exam page. After the professor returned the tests, the student filled in the correct answers, added some red pen marks, and then complained that the professor had failed to record a score for what appeared to be a completed exam. The culprit was discovered, however, when the professor had the red ink analyzed and proved that it came from a different pen than the one used to grade the other exams. Elsewhere, a student stole a notepad from her doctor's office, then used it to excuse herself from classes and to obtain makeup exams and extensions on papers.

Schools are having difficulty keeping up with dishonest students. Boston University launched a lawsuit against several Internet essay mills charging them with wire fraud, mail fraud, and racketeering. Many exam halls make students sit in alphabetical order to reduce the odds of cheaters sitting next to accomplices. These same students will be our lawyers, doctors, teachers, bankers, and ministers.

If you were one of the Boston University officials, what would you do in this situation? List two or three things you might do.

1. _____

2. _____

3. _____

8. Commitment to Ourselves

In a time when many students find it difficult to keep commitments to others, it is not surprising that students also have trouble keeping commitments to themselves. Mention a "New Year's Resolution" and you will likely be met with snickering. It is an accepted fact that resolutions made with the best intentions on January 1 are unlikely to last to January 31. When we determine to lose weight, get in shape, or pray regularly, we do so knowing that these actions would benefit us. Then the temptations come in rapid succession. Life gets busy. We find that none of our friends are doing what we are. Some feel that by merely acknowledging a behavior is good, it is almost the same as implementing the change in their lives. A woman once told me, "It's not hard to quit smoking. I should know. I've done it seven times."

Summary

Making a commitment to God according to the world's terms will be no better than those would-be disciples in Jesus' day whom He chastised, "Why do you call me, 'Lord, Lord' and do not do what I say?" (Luke 6:46). These people mentally asserted the value of obeying God but never followed through with a life of obedience.

The only way our promises to God will be realized is when we make commitments the way God does. When we refuse to go back on our word; when we place the integrity of our lives behind every promise; when we relentlessly persist until everything we promised God comes to fruition; then we will be in a position for God to perform a transforming work in us that will make us seekers of the cross.

Reflecting on the Cross and Our Commitments

As you surveyed typical commitments made in the Bible and in the secular world, God may have revealed to you that your commitments are more like the world's than like Christ's. Take a moment to hold your present commitments as a CrossSeeker against the standard of the cross.

1. Recall a commitment you made to your parents. Are you keeping it?

2. a) What commitments have you made to your boyfriend/girlfriend or spouse?
   b) How would Christ view the way you have been keeping your commitments to those you care about? ❑ Pleased ❑ Not Pleased

3. Think of a spoken or unspoken commitment you made to a friend. How would Jesus evaluate your faithfulness to your friends?

4. What commitment have you made to your employer? Does your job performance honor God?

5. a) What are some ethical commitments you have made to God, yourself, or significant others, such as being honest, giving your best, etc.?
   b) Are there other ethical commitments God wants you to implement in your life?

6. a) What are two commitments you have made to your church? Are you honoring those commitments?
   b) Are there other commitments you feel Christ would want you to make to your church?

Prayer of Commitment (Put in your own words, if you like.)

> *Dear Lord,*
> *Forgive me for using the world's standard instead of Yours for my life. Forgive me for making commitments to You, to others, and to myself, and then not keeping them. Reveal to me every area of my life where I have not been consistent, and help me to live my life with integrity. Amen.*

Chapter 4

INTEGRITY

STANDING BEFORE THE CROSS: A CRUCIFIED LIFE

"Do your best to present yourself to God as one approved, a workman who does not need to be ashamed and who correctly handles the word of truth." 2 Timothy 2:15

My attitudes and actions reveal my commitment to live the kind of life Christ modeled for me—to speak the truth in love, to stand firm in my convictions, to be honest and trustworthy.

CHAPTER 4

At 4:30 a.m. someone pounded on the door of Dr. Samuel A. Mudd's home. The physician listened to the man on his doorstep explain how his traveling companion had fallen from his horse en route to Washington and had badly injured his leg. The doctor invited them in. For the remainder of the day he tended to the wounded leg and allowed the men to rest. By 5 p.m., they were gone. That event would forever change the doctor's life and reputation. Dr. Mudd had tended to John Wilkes Booth, Abraham Lincoln's assassin. As a result, the saying, "Your name is mud," was born. Mudd spent four years in prison before receiving a pardon. Mudd died 14 years later at age 49, due partly to the yellow fever he contracted in prison. Over the next century, Mudd's descendants bore his shame. Finally, they launched a lawsuit hoping to clear their name of the notoriety inherited from Dr. Mudd.

As Christians and CrossSeekers, we have inherited a name, too—the name of Christ our Lord. This name is not associated with shame, but with honor. Christ is the pacesetter for the Christian life; He sets the example we must follow if we are to be like Him and bear His name in truth.

FOCUS ON THE CROSS

The cross is history's greatest event. God's plan to save people from their sin required a blameless, sinless sacrifice. He turned to His Son. Jesus had to experience humanity, its temptations and its suffering in order to become the perfect sacrifice God required. By His suffering and ultimately by His obedience, Jesus was prepared to pay the full penalty for our sin.

"During the days of Jesus' life on earth, he offered up prayers and petitions with loud cries and tears to the one who could save him from death, and he was heard because of his reverent submission. Although he was a son, he learned obedience from what he suffered and, once made perfect, he became the source of eternal salvation for all who obey him and was designated by God to be high priest in the order of Melchizedek. . . Such a high priest meets our need— one who is holy, blameless, pure, set apart from sinners, exalted above the heavens. Unlike the other high priests, he does not need to offer sacrifices day after day, first for his own sins, and then for the sins of the people. He sacrificed for their sins once for all when he offered himself. For the law appoints as high priests men who are weak; but the oath, which came after the law, appointed the Son, who has been made perfect forever" (Hebrews 5:7-10; 7:26-28).

Christ's obedience to His Father ultimately led Him to the cross as atonement for our sin. The writer of Hebrews observed that once the Father had fashioned His Son into the Savior, He was "perfect, holy, blameless, pure, and exalted." His character perfectly matched His assignment.

Integrity

Integrity is a popular word today. It means "original, uncorrupted, perfect, whole, complete." It describes something which holds true to its original design and purpose, no distortions or impurities having contaminated it.

Can you give a one-sentence definition from your world on the campus of "integrity?" How would your friends define this term?

_____

_____

When Jesus accepted the daunting role of Savior, it was crucial that He live a life of integrity. His calling was holy; His life could be no less.

FOCUS ON OUR CRUCIFIED LIVES

God calls Christians to honor Him by living as Christ did. However, a vast chasm separates our sinful nature from Christ's character. Only a radical transformation of our hearts will enable us to live lives of Christian integrity. A non-Christian cannot live a Christian life. A moral life, yes. But only those who undergo new birth can experience God's transforming power which makes us like Christ. The only obstacle to the process is the sin that we hide in our hearts and minds. We will not glorify God if we insist on controlling our lives. There is just one way to live an authentic Christian life. Our sinful nature must be crucified. Then the Holy Spirit will live Christ's life through us.

Would you say your life up to this point reveals you are living a Christlike life? What can you do to seek to be closer to the cross? Write down a couple of thoughts.

1. _____

2. _____

In the News: Death Brings Life

In September 1997, according to a Canadian news report, surgeons at a Toronto hospital took a revolutionary step to save the life of their patient—they killed him. The patient suffered from a complicated aneurysm. Dr. Michael Tymianski explained: "After careful deliberation we believed that temporarily killing the patient was the safest way to get him home again." The surgical team lowered the patient's body temperature to 15 degrees Celsius, then stopped his heart for 18 minutes while they performed the delicate operation. Because this man was willing to die, he lived.

The paradox of the Christian life is this: As CrossSeekers we cannot live unless we die. Our self-centeredness, pride, bitterness, jealousy, lust, greed, and anger must all be discarded as God transforms us into the likeness of His Son.

A Self-Righteous Fanatic

Before he met Christ, the apostle Paul was a self-righteous, proud, ambitious, murdering religious fanatic. In Paul's spiritual blindness, he thought arresting and killing Christians would gain him God's favor. Then an encounter with Christ changed everything. Paul suddenly realized that the actions he took pride in were actually cause for shame (Philippians 3:7-8). Only after God removed Paul's pride, ambition, and self-centeredness and changed his heart could Paul's life glorify God. Paul described it this way:

"I have been crucified with Christ and I no longer live, but Christ lives in me" (Galatians 2:20).

"Therefore, if anyone is in Christ, he is a new creation; the old has gone, the new has come!" (2 Corinthians 5:17).

If we are to have integrity as Christians, we must allow God to challenge everything in us that stands in the way of our Christlikeness.

Scripture is filled with descriptions of what a Christian's life should be like. Some of these descriptions are given. See if you can match correctly the phrase with the scripture. Put the letter of the alphabet next to the correct phrase. The first one is done for you.

__a__ salt of the earth	a. Matthew 5:13
_____ light of the world	b. Romans 8:17
_____ disciples	c. Ephesians 2:19
_____ servants	d. Romans 8:16
_____ Jesus' friends	e. 2 Corinthians 5:17
_____ belonging to Jesus Christ	f. Romans 1:7
_____ loved by God	g. Matthew 5:14

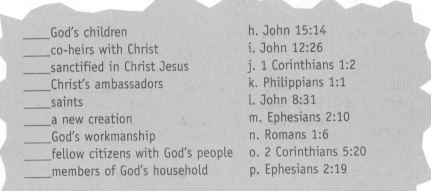

_____God's children
_____co-heirs with Christ
_____sanctified in Christ Jesus
_____Christ's ambassadors
_____saints
_____a new creation
_____God's workmanship
_____fellow citizens with God's people
_____members of God's household

h. John 15:14
i. John 12:26
j. 1 Corinthians 1:2
k. Philippians 1:1
l. John 8:31
m. Ephesians 2:10
n. Romans 1:6
o. 2 Corinthians 5:20
p. Ephesians 2:19

Key: a, g, i, l, h, n, f, d, b, j, o, k, e, m, p, c

This is only a sampling of the richness of our Christian inheritance as CrossSeekers. However, just because these things have been promised does not mean we are experiencing them. Only when we live with integrity will our lifestyle, our attitudes, and our walk with God be authentic.

Integrity on the job

I discovered the importance of integrity during a summer job. I was the only Christian working at a lumber yard for a demanding and intimidating boss. My boss was not a Christian, but he knew I was. One day $60.00 was missing from the cash register. Everyone at work was put on alert. The following Saturday, when the yard was full of customers, another $40.00 disappeared. Money began to disappear regularly, and it became obvious that it had to be an "inside job." Everyone was a suspect. The police were notified. The boss watched the cash register like a hawk, yet money continued to disappear. It infuriated him! Worker morale suffered as everyone asked himself, "Does the boss think I would steal from the company?" A few employees were told they could no longer use the cash register until the crimes were solved.

I wondered if my boss believed that, despite my Christianity, I was a thief. One day a co-worker assured me, "Don't worry. The boss doesn't suspect you. I overheard him telling his partner, 'You don't have to worry about Richard. He's a Christian. He wouldn't steal from us.'" What a relief that was! During those tense days of suspicion, I wondered if my actions had convinced anyone that I was a person of integrity. Now I knew they had. The manager eventually discovered the cash register was faulty. Whenever business was brisk and the pile of $20 bills grew high, bills would slip over the edge of the bin and be hidden inside the register. When the lost bills were discovered, every missing dollar was there. We were all cleared, but our integrity had certainly been scrutinized. How authentic a person of integrity are you? Check the following three areas to see God's model for authentic living.

1. Friend

Our lives must line up with our claims. We may claim the title of "friend" to Jesus. To us this may mean every time we have a problem, Jesus is instantly available to bail us out. We may believe that having Jesus as a friend means He will never chastise us. Jesus said:

"You are my friends *if you do what I command*" (John 15:14).

That's pretty straightforward. If you want to know if you are a friend of Jesus, ask yourself: "Do I do what He tells me to do?" On a scale of 1-10, with "10" being the best, put a mark on the scale closest to where you are in your walk with Christ in this area of your life.

0   1   2   3   4   5   6   7   8   9   10

2. Servant

Someone said, "I don't mind being called a servant; but I despise being treated like one!" If we are to hold this title with integrity, we must fulfill the requirements Jesus established.

He said:
"*Whoever serves me must follow me; and where I am, my servant also will be. My Father will honor the one who serves me*" (John 12:26).

As God's servants we must go where He asks us to go. If He asks for service in summer missions, we must do so or miss being on mission with God. We cannot be God's servants and yet serve on our terms. Jesus promised that if we follow Him, the Father will honor us. We will know we have been God's servants, because God will show us His pleasure with our lives.

On a scale of 1-10, with "10" being the best, put a mark on the scale closest to where you are in your walk with Christ in this area of your life.

0   1   2   3   4   5   6   7   8   9   10

3. Heir

Scripture says:

"The Spirit himself testifies with our spirit that we are God's children. Now if we are children, then we are heirs—heirs of God and co-heirs with Christ, if indeed we share in his sufferings in order that we may also share in his glory" (Romans 8:16-17).

What a privilege! Yet to claim this honored title of co-heirs with Christ, we must share in His suffering. Just as Christ gave His life to accomplish God's will, I, too, must be prepared to give my life completely to the Father's will, regardless of the inconvenience or suffering involved. How will I know when I have done this? The Holy Spirit will agree with my spirit that I am indeed God's child.

On a scale of 1-10, with "10" being the best, put a mark on the scale closest to where you are in your walk with Christ in this area of your life.

0	1	2	3	4	5	6	7	8	9	10

Amazing Grace!

John Newton is best known for the hymn "Amazing Grace." Newton was also a much-loved pastor in Olney, England and later in London. As a teenager, Newton was always in trouble. Falling in love with a young woman in Chatham, England, caused him to miss the ship that was to take him to a business career in Jamaica. Eventually he was pressed into the British navy aboard the ship Harwich. Still lovesick, John seized the first opportunity to desert. He was captured by a military patrol and strapped in irons. He was stripped, flogged, and forced into service on one of the most despised ships of his day—a slave-trading ship. Slaves were packed so tightly into the holds of the ships there was little room to move. Slaves were sexually abused by the crew. Beatings were frequent, disease was rampant, and many slaves died during the torturous voyages.

Newton indulged in every form of immorality and wickedness. He eventually became captain of a slave-trading ship. Newton's life was so despicable that only spiritual death could transform him into the saint he became. His pride and immorality had to die so God could change his heart. Thus, the once vile rebel became the humble servant who could gratefully write: *"Amazing grace! how sweet the sound, That saved a wretch* like me! I once was lost, but now am found, Was blind, but now I see." The old Newton died so the new Newton could live.

Many would-be Christians want to skip spiritual death and go directly to eternal life. This is not possible, for Christianity is not an additive. You cannot add Christ to your sinful life to make things run more smoothly. Once you have accepted Christ as Lord, it is impossible to "do business as usual." Christ is all-consuming. *When He enters your life, He takes center stage. Everything changes!*

CrossQuote

When He enters your life, He takes center stage. Everything changes!

We cannot live the Christian life fully, yet refuse to forgive. Our Christian lives will lack integrity if we harbor racist attitudes or prejudice. We can never be the saints God wants to make us if we continue to fill our minds with pornography. The apostle Paul died to his old ways. So did John Newton. We, too, must undergo spiritual death and allow the Holy Spirit to remove every attitude, desire, or habit which is inconsistent with our calling as Christ's disciples. Genuine conversion is much more than saying a prayer, walking the aisle, signing a card, or being baptized—it is a new birth.

It's easy to fool ourselves. Since we carry the label "Christian," or "CrossSeeker" we may assume we are living the Christian life. Because we were baptized or we attend church, or because we are relatively moral, we might presume our lives hold spiritual integrity. In fact, even as CrossSeekers, we must return often to the cross and allow Christ to measure our lives by His standards. Perhaps our exposure to the cross will reveal that what we say we believe is far removed from the way we actually live. Maybe we've tried to live the Christian life without giving anything up, without dying to ourselves, without allowing God to change us. Christ gave up *everything* to please His Father. We, too, must strive for such obedience if we are to live with integrity.

Whose ox have I taken?

The Bible gives an example of one man's integrity. As Samuel neared the end of his life, he initiated a time of accountability with those he had worked and lived with. These are his words:

> "Here I stand. Testify against me in the presence of the Lord and his anointed. Whose ox have I taken? Whose donkey have I taken? Whom have I cheated? Whom have I oppressed? From whose hands

have I accepted a bribe to make me shut my eyes? If I have done any of these, I will make it right."

"You have not cheated or oppressed us," they replied. "You have not taken anything from anyone's hand" (1 Samuel 12:3-4).

Now that's integrity! After spending his entire life among the Israelites, Samuel could face them eye to eye and challenge even one of them to prove that he had acted without virtue. What confidence! His example challenges me to consider whether I would dare to gather my family, friends, co-workers, and neighbors and challenge them to cite a time when I had not been completely above reproach in relating to them. As a CrossSeeker, are these areas you need to work on to glorify Christ?

It's too late for most of us to match Samuel's perfect record. We've already blown it too many times. Thankfully, God is more concerned with the present than our past. We can only repent of past mistakes and seek forgiveness from those we have offended. We can, however, change the way we live today.

Our problem so often is that we refuse to acknowledge the inconsistencies in our lives. We believe we are living above reproach despite evidence to the contrary. At times God has to get our attention before we will come to grips with the sin in our lives.

Changed Through Racquetball

I grew up with three brothers and a sister and quickly learned how to compete. I loved to *win!* As a child, I would do almost anything to win— including occasionally cheating. After graduating from college, I attended seminary to prepare for the ministry. I enjoyed playing racquetball at the seminary. I especially enjoyed winning. One day I was playing with some friends, and I made a questionable play. One friend became angry and loudly accused me of cheating. I was embarrassed and angry. How dare he accuse me like that! Here I was, a moral person, regularly attending church, reading my Bible, praying, and training to become a pastor. How could he call me a cheat? Later that day, I tried to pray, but I was still irritated. I asked God, "How could he accuse me of such things?" God's silence was deafening. I sensed God saying, "Richard, you don't always live your life wholly above reproach. You and I both know that below your religious exterior are some ugly things in your heart and mind." I was crushed. God was right. I looked pretty good on the outside, but I knew God saw my heart, and some of what was in there was not very pretty. If I wanted to be a minister for Christ, one with integrity that is, some things in my life would have go. I confessed my known sins to God, and I asked God to make me consistent on the inside with what I tried to project on the outside. Through the disturbing accusations of a friend, I experienced one of the greatest spiritual revivals in my life.

REFLECTING ON THE CROSS AND OUR CRUCIFIED LIVES

Just as it took an accusation to make me aware of inconsistencies in my life, perhaps because you have signed the CrossSeekers Covenant, your integrity has been recently questioned. You may have assumed all was well until you took an honest look at yourself. There are many clues that can reveal a lack of integrity. These include:

1. You have no close friends

2. You have difficulty holding a job

3. It seems someone is always angry with you

4. People are unwilling to lend you money or things

5. Others joke about how undependable you are

6. You are rarely on time

7. You consistently make lower grades than you could

8. People seem reluctant to give you responsibilities

9. People rarely seem to take you seriously

These are some signs that your life lacks integrity. Don't be like the woman who said to me: "If you want to know about marriage, ask me. I should know, I've been married five times!" The evidence screamed out that she knew little about marriage, but she failed to notice the obvious discrepancy between her words and her life.

If you are going to be a person of integrity, there must be consistency between your claims and your actions.

Respond to the following:

I am honest
    ❑ always   ❑ usually   ❑ sometimes   ❑ rarely
I give my best effort at work
    ❑ always   ❑ usually   ❑ sometimes   ❑ rarely
I strive to be above reproach in the way I relate to my boyfriend/girl-friend
    ❑ always   ❑ usually   ❑ sometimes   ❑ rarely
I never take things that do not belong to me
    ❑ always   ❑ usually   ❑ sometimes   ❑ rarely
The image I project lines up with who I really am
    ❑ always   ❑ usually   ❑ sometimes   ❑ rarely
I am not ashamed of how I talk about others when they are not present
    ❑ always   ❑ usually   ❑ sometimes   ❑ rarely
People can count on me
    ❑ always   ❑ usually   ❑ sometimes   ❑ rarely
People know I will treat them with respect
    ❑ always   ❑ usually   ❑ sometimes   ❑ rarely

As you considered the above statements, were you pleased with your response? If you were uncomfortable with some of the statements, there may be attitudes and habits in your life that need correction. Make a list of those things God is asking you to change in your life. Pray daily for God to remove these sinful habits or attitudes from your life and to show you what actions you need to take to become like Christ. Remember, being a CrossSeeker is not a destination. It's a journey with Christ. Share what God is telling you with trusted friends and ask them to hold you accountable to obey what God is telling you to do. When you allow Christ to remove those things which are inconsistent with His character, you will be able to truly live your life with integrity.

Prayer of Commitment (Put in your own words.)

If you are serious about giving God complete control over every area of your life, begin by praying this prayer:

Dear Lord,

*Please forgive me for selfishly trying to hold on to parts of my life without giving them over to You. I have tried to be a Christian and yet hold on to my sin, and I realize I cannot do that. I want my life to please You, and I am willing for You to take any sinful thought, habit, attitude, desire, ambition, relationship, or lust in my life and put it to death. **I commit myself** to become like Christ, and no matter how painful, to have You remove anything that is not consistent with Christ. Amen.*

I desire to be a person of INTEGRITY!

SPIRITUAL GROWTH

TAKING UP YOUR CROSS: BECOMING LIKE CHRIST

*"So then, just as you received Christ Jesus as Lord,
continue to live in Him, rooted and built up in
Him, strengthened in the faith as you were taught,
and overflowing with thankfulness."*
Colossians 2:6-7

The Christian life is a continuing journey,
and I am committed to a consistent, personal
relationship with Jesus Christ, to faithful study
of His word, and to regular corporate spiritual
growth through the ministry of the
New Testament church.

In the News: Too Much To Drink

Twenty-two year old Dwayne Green was a would-be thief who thought he had a foolproof plan. He staked out a house where the residents were away for the weekend—an easy heist. He quickly gained entry and began piling electronic equipment and jewelry by the front door. Then he spied a bottle of whiskey. Unable to resist, he took a swig. He continued drinking while he worked. Eventually the liquor took its toll. Overcome with drowsiness, Green decided to lie down for a moment on the owner's bed. Minutes later, the newspaper account states, he was awakened by a policeman, thanks to the summons of an alert neighbor. Police nicknamed him the "Goldilocks bandit." Dwayne Green learned that attempting a serious task in a casual manner can have disastrous results.

Sincere Christians want to be more committed, so they make innumerable resolutions. Plans for daily Bible reading and prayer are often at the center of our commitments. We frequently resolve to get more involved in church or to be more active in personal evangelism. We make plans with honorable intent. Nevertheless, we often fail. Like the "Goldilocks bandit," well-meaning Christians and CrossSeekers become distracted and are rudely awakened only to realize their well-made plans have come to naught.

Christ does not save you from your sins so you can do the right things. He saves you for a relationship. It's easy to become sidetracked. That's why it is so critical to keep your eyes on Christ. It is the cross that keeps your life in proper perspective. Have you been "caught napping" in your relationship with Christ? Or have you been purposefully and steadily growing in your walk with Him?

FOCUS ON THE CROSS

Jesus' primary mission was not to heal the sick, to feed the hungry, or to preach to the multitudes—it was to die on the cross for the sins of humanity. Everything else was a prelude to His crucifixion. It is incomprehensible that God chose the cross as the means for His Son's death. Of all the instruments of execution known in the First Century, there was none more despised than crucifixion.

Greek and Roman citizens were exempt from crucifixion, as the Romans considered it a punishment fitting only for slaves and rebels. Cicero, the Roman orator, was so appalled by crucifixion that he urged: "Let every name of the cross be far away not only from the body of a Roman Citizen, but even from his thoughts." Josephus, the Jewish historian, described crucifixion as "the most wretched of deaths."

The usual procedure for crucifixion began with torture. Roman soldiers flogged the prisoner, weakening him, so death by crucifixion did not take as long as it might otherwise. After the whipping, the prisoner was forced to carry the crosspiece through the streets to the place of crucifixion. Jesus was beaten so viciously He needed help to carry His cross.

At the place of crucifixion, the cross was laid on the ground and the prisoner stretched upon it. Generally, prisoners were tied to crosses, but Jesus was nailed to His (Luke 24:39; John 20:25). The cross was lifted up and dropped into its hole, jarring the occupant as it fell into place. A sign would often be nailed to the cross above the victim's head, proclaiming the crime for which he was being punished.

The suffering reached its climax as the prisoner hung on the cross. Death could take up to 36 hours. Prisoners felt the day's heat and the night's cold. Flies and insects would torment them. They could not attend to their bodily functions. Jeering crowds showed no concern for their agony. Jesus was crucified for the salvation of those who stood at the foot of His cross and ridiculed Him.

Death came by gradual suffocation. As the victim hung on the cross, it became increasingly difficult to breathe. Only by lifting himself up could the prisoner take a breath. If the prisoner were physically strong, he might survive the crucifixion. If that were the case, the executioner would break his legs. Thus disabled, the prisoner would suffocate quickly.

Much of the despicable nature of the cross was its public shame. As people watched the prisoner carrying his cross, everyone knew his life would soon be over. There were no further courts of appeal. There was no escape. His immediate future was suffering and death. Once a person died on the cross, his corpse was often left for days as a grim reminder of the consequences of his crime. Nothing was more horrible to a pious Jew, since Scripture indicated that an exposed corpse meant that person was cursed by God (Deuteronomy 21:22-23).

God might have chosen another method to satisfy His requirement for atonement of man's sin. Mysteriously, He allowed His Son to be humiliated and tortured in a most barbaric manner. The absolute horror of the cross reflects God's abhorrence of sin, the heinous nature of sin, and the length to which God would go to save us.

Take a moment to meditate upon the fact that Jesus was willing to endure this horrific suffering because He loved you. Consider the awesome sacrifice Christ made so He might save you from your sin. Share it with another student if you can.

FOCUS ON FOLLOWING CHRIST

You may find the story of the cross disturbing. Even more unsettling is that Jesus set His crucifixion as the pattern for anyone seeking to be His disciple:

> *"If anyone would come after me, he must deny himself and take up his cross and follow me. For whoever wants to save his life will lose it, but whoever loses his life for me will find it. What good will it be for a man if he gains the whole world, yet forfeits his soul? Or what can a man give in exchange for his soul? For the Son of Man is going to come in his Father's glory with his angels, and then he will reward each person according to what he has done"* (Matthew 16:24-27).

His point is crystal clear. The Christian and CrossSeekers life is more than attending church services, saying prayers, reading the Bible, giving money, or becoming a missionary. Of course these are important, but they are not the essence of Christianity. The CrossSeekers life centers on following Christ. It is a personal, intimate, growing relationship with the person Jesus Christ. It is really quite simple. Follow and obey Jesus. Make a commitment to consistent spiritual growth. Jesus outlined it as a three-step process.

1. Deny Yourself

The world urges you to affirm yourself; Jesus commands the opposite. He does not mean berate, humiliate, or starve yourself. Nor does He ask you to deny yourself all pleasure. To deny self is not to deny your inherent worth as a child of God. Rather, self-denial involves rejecting the temptation to allow sin to control you. It comprises the choice to yield every part of your life to Christ. Scripture says that we have all "fallen short" of God's standard and no one naturally chooses to do what is right (Romans 3:12, 23). Because we gravitate toward sin, we must resist our tendencies and relinquish total control to Christ.

We cannot remain self-centered and follow Jesus as Lord. We cannot stay where we are and go with Jesus. We cannot follow our standard and fulfill God's. Either we deny ourselves, or we deny God.

I've met people who wanted to follow Jesus, but were unwilling to deny self. Here is their reasoning:

"I want Jesus as my Lord, but I have a relationship I can't give up."

"I'd like to do whatever God asks, but I could never live there."

"I want to obey Christ, but I can't forgive that person after what he did to me!"

"I realize I should stop this sin, but I've been doing it so long I don't think I can."

"I have my career planned, and I can't see Jesus asking me to change."

In other words, "I know Jesus should be the Lord of my life and that's fine, as long as He never tells me to do anything I don't want to do!"

Self-Denial at the Olympics

Eric Liddell's story became famous through the award-winning movie, Chariots of Fire. Liddell was a gifted British athlete, highly favored to win the 100-meter sprint in the 1924 Olympics in Paris. Liddell had trained strenuously. His country was counting on him to bring home the gold medal. International fame and prestige would be his along with congratulations from the king. While training for the event, Liddell learned the race was scheduled for a Sunday. This presented a dilemma. He believed that Sunday was a day to worship God, not to strive for personal glory. The world told him that he owed it to himself and his country to win the victory and become a hero. When Liddell announced he would deny himself the almost certain prospect of a gold medal in order to honor God, his unusual decision made headlines worldwide!

Four days later, Liddell won gold and set a new world record in a race he did not usually run—the 400 meter sprint. Characteristically, rather than basking in his success, he set off for China as a missionary. This famous athlete spent the remainder of his life serving God. When the Japanese armies invaded China during World War II, Liddell was captured and interned in a prison camp. Only two months before the end of the war, Liddell, 43, died of a brain tumor in a squalid prisoner-of-war camp far from his family. The world does not understand this kind of self-denial, but it is the only kind worthy of Christ.

Think of how Liddell's life reflected spiritual growth. Jot down at least three things you recognize:

1. _____

2. _____

3. _____

Western society is obsessed with rights. These rights include such things as a job, an education, respect, sexual indulgence, freedom to own a gun, taking one's own life, or taking the life of an unborn baby. This emphasis on rights has permeated Christian thinking. There are those who feel that Christians have the right to a comfortable lifestyle, marriage, children, a house, residence in a part of the country they enjoy, living near parents, and freedom from discomfort. While these things are not wrong to enjoy, Christians must acknowledge that Christ holds the rights to their lives. We cannot claim anything for ourselves except that which God gives us by His grace.

2. Take up Your Cross

Jesus insists that to grow spiritually, His disciples take up their cross. The significance of this command was not lost on the twelve. They knew well what carrying a cross entailed. They had seen condemned men carrying their crosses through the streets. They had watched men die on crosses. The disciples understood that once you took up your cross, there was no laying it down. Once you began carrying your cross, future plans became irrelevant. Any bitterness toward another was meaningless. Any lust or ambition was futile. Once a person began carrying his cross, his life was no longer his own.

A Living Martyr

During the persecution of Christians under the Roman empire, thousands were killed for their faith in Christ. Under the emperor Septimus Severus, a violent persecution swept across the empire in 202 A.D. In the city of Alexandria, Egypt, this persecution was wrought with a vengeance. A Christian named Leonides was arrested and taken away to be burned at the stake. His son, Origen, was so inspired by his father's willingness to give his life for Christ that Origen determined to give his life to the flames as well. Sensing her son's noble intentions, Origen's resourceful mother hid his clothes. When Origen prepared to dress to present himself to the magistrate, he discovered he had no clothes. By the time Origen had found them, God had shown him how he could serve Him as a living martyr, rather than ending his life by execution.

Origen lived the rest of his life as though he had died that day. He became one of the Fathers of the early church, and God used him mightily to impact the lives of many people. In 250 A.D., the Roman Emperor Decius launched a new campaign of persecution against Christians. Origen was imprisoned and endured an iron collar. He was locked in stocks in the dungeon and beaten. Origen had lived as a martyr for so long that he was able to endure torture when the time for his persecution finally came.

How is Origen's example beneficial for today's students? _____

_____

_____

Many students are confused about what it means to "take up your cross." Some think it means displaying signs of their faith, like wearing a cross on a necklace or putting a bumper sticker on their car. Others think it is the suffering they go through, such as when their parents divorce or when their boss treats them unfairly. Some behave as if their cross is something that waits to be picked up as they enter the church building and to be placed by the church door as they leave. Some people in the Philippines actually allow themselves to be temporarily nailed to crosses over the Easter season in order to identify with Christ.

Biblically, a cross is taken up by choice. No one can make you pick up the cross of Christ, and no one can do it for you. The cross is not so much a symbol of Christian suffering as it is a symbol that Christians have yielded total control of their lives to Christ. No one can make you become a CrossSeeker. No one can become one for you!

3. Follow Christ

Andrew received an unsettling response from Jesus when he first met Him. After listening to the popular teacher speak, Andrew saw Jesus departing, and he asked Him, "Rabbi, where are you staying?" Andrew and his companion were curious about Jesus. They wondered where He stayed at night, where He was going, what He was really like. Rather than answering his question directly, Jesus issued an invitation: "Come . . . and you will see" (John 1:39). Andrew learned that the only way to get to know Jesus was to be with Him. His invitation was simple:

"Follow Me and find out!" That's where faith operates. Generally, we like to know our destination before we begin a journey. We like to know the cost in time and money before we commit ourselves. It takes tremendous faith to say to Jesus: "I will follow You and not worry about where You lead. I will follow You, even though I know You may lead me through suffering or persecution. I will follow You, even though You may ask me to do things I have despised or feared. You may take me right past things I have always hoped for, but I will trust that You know what is best."

It is tempting for a CrossSeeker to limit Christian experience to learning about Jesus. That won't do. We must go where He goes. Christ will never tell us everything that the future holds. If He did, we would put our trust in our knowledge of the future instead of in Him. He wants us to focus on Him as He leads us daily, so that we come to experience Him as we seek and walk with Him.

A Personal Struggle

I grew up in a pastor's home. As a child, one of my favorite games was "church." I was the pastor, and my brother, Tom, led the worship. We sat on my top bunk and conducted the service. My mother, sitting in a chair below, was the congregation. Tom would lead her in singing "Jesus Loves Me" and then I would open my Bible and wax eloquent on the evils of spanking children. My mother would faithfully rededicate herself to try harder in the future. Her commitment never lasted very long.

Playing church was fun as long as it was just a game. But when I entered college, I sensed God really was calling me to be a pastor. It scared me to death! I had seen the sacrifices my father had made as a pastor. I watched him work long, tiring, often thankless hours for very little pay. I knew that to be a pastor meant spending much time in prayer and Bible study. I knew it meant living a godly lifestyle others could model.

I resisted what I sensed God was asking me to do. I reasoned: I have been a moral, Christian teenager thus far, and I deserve to have some fun without always having to be deadly earnest about my Christian life. I didn't plan on doing drugs or breaking the law, I just wanted to enjoy life for a while. I continued with regular church attendance and my involvement in student ministries on campus, but didn't listen too closely to God, because I suspected what He would tell me.

One evening a friend came to see my brothers and me. He was in distress. Satan seemed to have him in a vice grip from which he could not escape. My brothers and I realized that he needed spiritual help, so we prayed. I will never forget the sense of being absolutely powerless as I prayed. It was as if my prayers were merely bouncing off the ceiling and never reaching God. I became painfully aware of how carelessly I had treated my relationship with Christ. I had merely been going through the motions. I had no spiritual power, no effective prayer life, no Bible knowledge that could help my friend. It became apparent that my careless attitude toward God's leading meant I was ill-prepared to help the needy friend He sent my way. That was a life-changing moment. I resolved that I would get serious about my relationship with the Lord. I stopped worrying about where Christ might lead me and started obeying every time I knew He was asking me to follow Him.

The next Sunday I stood before my church and told them about accepting God's call to be a pastor. As I sat down, a friend stood to confess that he, too, had been resisting God's call into the ministry. Then others stood to testify the same thing. I realized that my resistance to take up my cross and follow Christ had been a negative influence on many others. Once I got my life right with Christ, He used my example to inspire others to do the same.

After reading of my personal struggle, what are the key elements where you see me wanting to do things my way?_____

_____

What are the key elements which demonstrate God was in control of my struggle?_____

_____

Which part of the struggle do you most relate to at this point in your spiritual journey?_____

_____

You may know exactly what Christ is telling you to do, but like I was, you are afraid of the cost. You fear that Christ might call you to go somewhere or do something you don't want to do. Go back and stand before the cross. Watch Jesus dying there for you. Remember the suffering He endured so God might give you eternal life. Then listen to Christ's invitation to deny yourself, take up your cross, and follow Him. As a CrossSeeker, do you really have a choice?

In The News: A Long-Term Commitment

Shoiki Yokoi was a tailor in 1941 when he was drafted into the Japanese Imperial Army. According to a news story in the Calgary Herald, he was sent to Guam during the final stages of the war. During the American invasion of Guam, most of the 22,000 Japanese soldiers defending the island were killed, but Yokoi fled into the jungle, where he refused to surrender. Unaware of the war's end, he lived in a cave and ate fruit, fish, rats, and frogs. Upon his discovery in 1972, he returned to Japan. His first words were, "It is with much embarrassment that I return." Yokoi said he felt remorse for hiding and not serving his emperor more faithfully.

In a similar newspaper story, Lieutenant Hiroo Onada was stationed in the Philippines during World War II. He and two companions continued to wage war against the local inhabitants long after the war ended. One soldier was killed in a gun battle in 1945. A second companion was killed in 1972. Finally, in 1974, Japan sent Onada's former World War II commanding officer to the Philippine jungle, and over a loudspeaker, he commanded Onada to give up his fight. Onada emerged from the jungle on March 10, 1974, wearing his much-repaired Imperial Army uniform.

Both men had received orders from their superiors, and they were determined to obey them, no matter what the cost and no matter how long it took! Even when they were all alone, they refused to abandon their task. If such long-term commitment is given to a lost cause, how much more tenacious ought we to be as we follow Christ, who has already won the victory over sin and death?

Reflecting on Taking Up Your Cross

Reflect on the following questions. (Circle the appropriate response.)

1. Have I completely denied myself?

   ❑ Yes   ❑ Almost   ❑ I'm trying
   ❑ Rarely   ❑ Never

2. Are there areas of my life which I still want to control?

   ❑ Yes   ❑ Almost   ❑ I'm trying
   ❑ Rarely   ❑ Never

3. Am I confident that I am presently where Christ wants me
   to be spiritually?

   ❑ Yes   ❑ Almost   ❑ I'm trying
   ❑ Rarely   ❑ Never

4. Am I reluctant to go anywhere Christ might lead me?

   ❑ Yes   ❑ Almost   ❑ I'm trying
   ❑ Rarely   ❑ Never

Prayer of Commitment (Put it in your own words.)

Dear Lord,

Forgive me for not trusting You with my life. I have been affirming myself, my desires, and my ambitions instead of denying them. I have been reluctant to take up my cross, because I have feared the cost. I have not followed You when I knew You were leading me where I needed to go. Please help me to deny everything in my life that is not bringing You glory. Help me as a CrossSeeker to say:

*I commit myself
to daily deny myself,
take up my cross,
and follow You wherever
You lead me.
Amen.*

WITNESS

CARRYING YOUR CROSS BEFORE OTHERS: A CHRISTLIKE WITNESS

"Always be prepared to give an answer to anyone who asks you to give the reason for the hope that you have."
1 Peter 3:15

I will tell others the story of how Jesus changed my life and I will seek to live a radically change life each day. I will share the good news of Jesus Christ with courage and boldness.

Love Letters

During one of my summer jobs as a college student, I worked at a factory which made prefabricated homes. It was a huge complex with work stations scattered throughout. The company paid low wages and employed several minimum-security prisoners who were bussed to the site each day and then returned to the prison at night. I worked with several of these convicts.

My future wife, Lisa, worked in the executive offices of the same company. Lisa and I were not yet officially dating. We considered ourselves "just friends." Lisa finished work by 5:00 p.m. and left for home, while my shift lasted until 11:30 p.m. To my delight, Lisa would leave notes on my windshield for me to pick up as I was leaving work each evening. One day I realized I could go out to my car during my break at 7:00 p.m. and read her note then. One of my prisoner co-workers noticed me returning from the parking lot with a huge smile on my face. He knew something was up. The next night he followed me and discovered my secret. The following night, when the lunch-break horn sounded, this guy sprinted to my car and grabbed my note! He headed for the warehouse with the intention of reading it aloud. I had other plans. I lunged for him and brought him down in the parking lot. The rest of the crew sensed some excitement and gathered around, chanting, "Fight! Fight! Fight!" To my dismay, the love-note thief crammed the piece of paper into his mouth, muttering, "Let's see you get this!" It never even slowed me down. I wrapped my hands around his throat and began to squeeze. He spit out the note, coughing and gasping for air. I seized my soggy prize. It was a bit chewed up, but still readable. The precious message was mine!

As CrossSeekers, we have received a love message more precious than any summer romance note. Yet at times, CrossSeekers treat God's message in the same way I treated my notes from Lisa—as something just for me, as something I am reluctant to share with anyone else. God's loving relationship with us is something He expects us to share with others. Second Corinthians 3:1-3 explains that Christians are God's messages of love. If people want to know about God's love, they only have to read what God has written across our lives. Wherever we go, we ought to be God's love letter to those around us. As CrossSeekers we should speak and live a relevant, authentic, and consistent witness.

What is the importance of a "love letter" to you? Check all which apply:
- ❑ very important   ❑ waste of time   ❑ never look at it
- ❑ personal and not to be shared   ❑ very affirming
- ❑ waste of paper   ❑ needs to be shared   ❑ other

Telling others about Christ has eternal significance. Yet many Christians and CrossSeekers frequently struggle with witnessing. Commitments to witness to others are often made and often broken. The best place to begin in examining our commitment to evangelism is the cross.

Focus on the Cross: The Witness of Christ

Jesus' entire life on earth focused on the cross. Even before His birth, the angels instructed Joseph: "You are to give him the name Jesus, because he will save his people from their sins" (Matthew 1:21). Jesus' baptism foreshadowed His death on the cross. It would be at the cross that God's message of salvation would be most clearly told.

A battle-hardened centurion stood by the cross where Jesus was crucified. Centurions were placed in command at crucifixions and were responsible to see that no one freed the prisoner and that the condemned were put to death. The centurion at Jesus' crucifixion would have seen hundreds of deaths. He watched men suffer agonizing pain in their final hours. He had listened to many beg for mercy and others curse the spectators who watched them suffer. Many entered eternity bitter at their fate. This veteran soldier assumed the execution of Jesus and the other two would be no different. One of the thieves died, defiant to the end. The other was remorseful for his actions. But the man crucified in the middle was unlike any man the centurion had seen before. Despite His agony, there was a serenity about Him which others lacked. While people mocked Him, He asked God to forgive them. Although He was suffering a humiliating death, He seemed victorious. As this prisoner came to the end of His life, He cried out triumphantly, "It is finished!" Upon Jesus' death, the sky darkened, and the earth trembled. This veteran centurion standing at the foot of the cross proclaimed: "Surely this man was the son of God!" (Mark 15:39). Witnessing Jesus' death convinced the cynical centurion that Jesus truly was who He said He was.

Jesus said: "But I, when I am lifted up from the earth, will draw all men to myself" (John 12:32). He was foretelling the manner of His death. It is also true that when His name is lifted up before others, college students will be attracted to Him. As hideous as crucifixion was, picturing

Jesus on the cross is a vivid reminder that God loves us and has provided for our sin. The call to Jesus' disciples and CrossSeekers is to lift up the name of Jesus at every opportunity, so others may be drawn to Him. When Jesus told His disciples to "take up their crosses," He was asking them to publicly demonstrate that they were His followers. Just as it was impossible to carry a cross through the streets of the city and be inconspicuous, so it is impossible to truly follow Christ and not publicly claim Him before others.

As the apostle Paul related to people, he chose to "know nothing . . . except Jesus Christ and him crucified" (1 Corinthians 2:2). Everything Paul did was related to Jesus' death on the cross. Paul correctly predicted that when he lifted up the name of Jesus, he would receive two reactions. He observed: "For the message of the cross is foolishness to those who are perishing, but to us who are being saved it is the power of God" (1 Corinthians 1:18).

Paul knew not everyone would respond positively when he presented Christ to them. Some would react angrily and even attempt to kill him. Paul also understood that his role was not to convict people of their sin. His job was to bring Christ to everyone's attention and allow the Holy Spirit to convict them of their sin and to draw them to Christ. Likewise, it is not our job to make students or people we associate with on a daily basis to become Christians. Our role is to lift up Christ at every opportunity. The Holy Spirit will convict them of their need for Christ.

Lifting Up Christ at 33,000 Feet

Here's an example of what I am sharing with you. A middle-aged woman sat next to me on a flight to Salt Lake City. We greeted each other, and in the course of our conversation I mentioned I was a minister. She quickly informed me that she had not been in church for many years, and God would probably not be pleased with the way she was presently living. When I told her God was prepared for her to return to Him, she simply shrugged and then ordered a drink from the stewardess. The woman poked fun at me for not drinking alcohol and offered to share her drink with me. While she was making light of my convictions, the captain's voice came over the intercom. He explained that the computer for the right engine was malfunctioning and would have to be shut down. In order to do that, the engine would first have to be turned off. To balance the plane's performance, they would go through the same procedure on the left computer and engine, and the pilot would fly the plane manually. The pilot said he was telling us this so if we experienced any excessive turbulence, we would know what was happening.

The woman beside me turned white. Capping her drink, she clutched my arm and hissed, "I knew it! As we were taxiing on the runway I thought the engine sounded funny!" Then she turned to me and pleaded: "Preacher, shouldn't you be praying?" For the rest of the flight, I told her how to find peace in Christ. As we parted, she promised to call upon a Christian friend and return to church.

As I had the opportunity to "lift up Christ" to this woman, I had no idea what would come of it. At first it appeared it would only bring me two hours of bad "preacher jokes!" But in God's mysterious way, He used an unsettling event to get a woman's attention, and He allowed me the privilege of speaking for Him.

What would you have said or done to share Christ with this woman?

1. _____

2. _____

3. _____

Focus on Our Christian Witness

Jesus commanded His disciples:

"You will be my witnesses in Jerusalem, and in all Judea and Samaria, and to the ends of the earth" (Acts 1:8).

Jesus likened being His disciple with being His witness. Jesus assumed that anyone who experienced a life-changing relationship with Him would want to tell others about it. They would want to tell people in their immediate relationships, in the city where they lived. They would want to talk about Jesus when they were in other parts of the country. Christians would share their faith with people of other cultures and lifestyles. Distance would not limit the witness of God's people. Jesus' disciples would be willing to leave their homes and families and go all over the world to tell others about Him. As a CrossSeeker and disciple of Christ, think about how much of your time is actually given to sharing your faith.

It may be through an FCA (Fellowship of Christian Athletes) group or a group from the BCM (Baptist Campus Ministry), but the one thing they have in common is the sharing of their witness to others.

Jot down two ways you see the witness of Jesus Christ shared on your campus.

1. _____

2. _____

Three Ways to Witness

It can be intimidating to witness to skeptical college students. When I was a student, my philosophy professor, an atheist, publicly ridiculed Christians in class. Students wore T-shirts with blasphemous sayings on them. Our Christian student organization held a forum on campus concerning cults, and a local cult sent people to fill up the chairs in the room and harass the speaker. During a Christian student social gathering, two students hostile to the gospel, dressed in bizarre costumes and attempted to disrupt the event. Numerous Christian groups have been harassed as they attempted to give free Bibles to students on campus. In such an environment, a Christian can easily become discouraged about witnessing for Christ. Yet Jesus assumed that telling others about Him would be a natural part of a Christian's lifestyle. It does not have to be complicated. There are at least three ways you can tell others about Christ.

1. Baptism

One way you can witness to others about your relationship with Christ is through your baptism. Paul explained spiritual baptism this way:

> *"We were therefore buried with him through baptism into death in order that, just as Christ was raised from the dead through the glory of the Father, we too may live a new life. . . our old self was crucified with him so that the body of sin might be done away with, that we should no longer be slaves to sin . . . . In the same way, count yourselves dead to sin but alive to God in Christ Jesus"* (Romans 6:4, 6, 11).

Jesus' public ministry began with His baptism. Observers did not realize it then, but Jesus' baptism foretold His death and resurrection. It became a symbol millions of believers would duplicate to identify with the saving work of Christ. Christians practice baptism as a symbol of what takes place in a new believer's life. Getting lowered into the water symbolizes the old, sinful person being lowered into a grave. Being raised out of the water pictures a new, forgiven person resurrected from spiritual death to new life. In New Testament times, Christians were often baptized in a river or in a pool of water. These were gathering places, which made baptism a public act, often before large crowds of unbelievers. To be baptized was to tell everyone in your community you had become a Christian. I know of two churches that did not have a church building with a baptistry, so they rented space in the community swimming pool. One church had to hire a lifeguard before they were allowed to immerse anyone in the public pool. The other church had to wait for the wave pool to be turned off before they could safely baptize. These public acts of baptism are probably more similar to the way it was done at the time of Christ. No matter how it is done, baptism is a time of joy in a new believer's life.

Sometimes baptisms are fraught with humor. A college student who was baptized in our church wore an oversized white shirt for the occasion. He was also wearing a T-shirt underneath with the large smiling face of a cartoon character on the front. As the student was raised out of the water to symbolize his new life, his outer shirt, now wet, became totally transparent. The congregation was greeted with a large cartoon face smiling brightly at them!

As a CrossSeeker or a new Christian, have you been baptized as a believer? If not, that is one of the first ways you can publicly witness to what God has done in your life. Some churches ask those being baptized to describe the difference Christ has made in their lives. At times, the simple drama of the baptism is enough to give a powerful message. Be sure to invite your family and friends who are not Christians. Your act of obedience may provide a compelling witness for them.

2. Lifestyle

To live with integrity, your walk must match your talk. This is true whether you are in a classroom or on the Internet. Can you claim to have the King of the universe dwelling within you, yet live a defeated life? *Can you maintain that the Holy Spirit controls your life if your lifestyle is immoral?* If you declare that God is all-powerful, yet you suffer from worry and fear, your anxiety invalidates your claim.

> ### CrossQuote
> *Can you maintain that the Holy Spirit controls your life if your lifestyle is immoral?*

When the disciples witnessed, they elicited an interesting response. Though not everyone agreed with their message, "When they saw the courage of Peter and John and realized that they were unschooled, ordinary men, they were astonished and they took note that these men had been with Jesus" (Acts 4:13). Jesus' disciples displayed a wisdom and power that could not be explained in human terms. The only apparent explanation for their extraordinary lives was that they had been with Jesus. There was a consistency between the message they shared and the courageous and miraculous way they lived their lives that convinced others of their claims.

In the book of Titus, Paul tells of some would-be Christians who "claim to know God, but by their actions they deny him" (Titus 1:16). The lives of these so-called Christians nullified everything they said about knowing Jesus. The CrossSeekers lifestyle is important. The way we live may not convince someone to become a Christian, but our inappropriate behavior can discourage someone from seeking our God. Perhaps no more stinging charge has been laid against the church than hypocrisy—that Christians say one thing but do another.

Integrity and Concrete

During my first three years of college, I worked for a bricklaying company every summer. Most of the men were nice enough, but none of them were Christians. Some used the most profane language I had ever heard! These men knew I was a Christian, and they enjoyed talking with me about my faith. When we were all crowded into the company truck driving to a work site, the boss would sometimes say, "Richard, talk to us about religion. I like it when you talk about religion!" As we talked, they would challenge me and try to find fault with what I was saying. They were also intrigued that I did not swear. They even suggested some relatively mild cuss words they thought I could use in order to fit in with them!

One day a load of concrete arrived at the job site. One of the men attempted to swing the chute located at the back of the truck around so the concrete could be emptied into a wheelbarrow. The chute was stuck. A second man tried unsuccessfully to loosen it. As they both went to find a tool, I stepped up to give it a try. I was wearing only shorts and work boots. With all my strength I pulled on the stubborn chute. Suddenly it gave way and whirled toward me. The metal edge gashed open my exposed leg, drawing blood immediately. I still remember the searing pain as I clenched my teeth to keep from shouting out. By the grace of God, I gained control over the pain and continued to work. As I released the concrete down the chute, I heard my boss utter an expletive. Surprised, I looked up and discovered him watching me from the scaffolding above. Afraid I had done something wrong, I asked, "What's wrong?"

Shaking his head he replied, "Don't you *ever* swear?"

I knew then that God had given me the strength to maintain my Christian witness even under the most trying circumstances. These men probably suspected it was not difficult to talk about my Christian commitment while driving comfortably in the company truck. It was quite different to maintain my convictions when I thought no one was watching and I was in pain. You don't always know when you are being watched. People are far more aware of your life than you might expect. If the witness you give with your mouth is going to have maximum effect, it will have to be matched with the integrity and witness of your life.

3. Verbal Witness

Three ways to verbally give witness about Christ are: a) your personal testimony; b) a biblical presentation; c) inviting others to respond to Christ.

a. Personal Testimony

Your personal testimony is your own story of how you came to know and follow Christ. This includes: what your life was like before you met Christ; how you discovered your *need* for Christ; and what your life has been like since you accepted Christ as your Lord and Savior. A personal testimony is not about everything there is to know about God. It simply tells your experience. If you were depressed and discouraged before you became a Christian, but you have experienced peace and joy since you met Christ, that is your testimony. As you relate this experience, others may challenge your interpretation of your experience, but they cannot refute your experience. Your task as a CrossSeeker and Christian is to bear witness of what has happened in your life and to lift up Jesus. The Holy Spirit will draw people to Him as they listen to you speak. Only He can convict people of their sin and transform their lives.

CrossQuote

"Whether he is a sinner or not, I don't know. One thing I do know. I was blind but now I see!"

(John 9:25).

A classic example of personal testimony came from a blind man to whom Jesus gave sight. Skeptics wanted to discredit Jesus and undermine His miracle. Religious authorities asked the healed man how Jesus did it, as well as theological questions he could not answer. Yet he could say: *"Whether he is a sinner or not, I don't know. One thing I do know. I was blind but now I see!"* (John 9:25). The skeptics couldn't argue with that.

Don't allow skeptics to diminish your testimony of what God has done for you. Write out your story so you can tell it in two minutes. You are the expert on what God has done in your life, so share it with confidence.

b. Biblical Presentation

A second way of verbally witnessing is through a biblical presentation of Christ. You may present Christ by telling people what the Bible says about Jesus and mankind's sinful condition. Several key verses are:

God's love for us:

".. . I have come that they may have life, and have it to the full" (John 10:10).

Humanity's sinful condition:

"For all have sinned and fall short of the glory of God" (Romans 3:23).

Punishment for sin:

"For the wages of sin is death, but the gift of God is eternal life in Christ Jesus our Lord" (Romans 6:23).

God's Answer for sin:

"But God demonstrates his own love for us in this: While we were still sinners, Christ died for us" (Romans 5:8).

Our response:

"If you confess with your mouth, 'Jesus is Lord,' and believe in your heart that God raised him from the dead, you will be saved" (Romans 10:9).

Our confidence:

"I write these things to you who believe in the name of the Son of God so that you may know that you have eternal life" (1 John 5:13).

These verses are worth memorizing. As a CrossSeeker, opportunities will come to tell someone about Jesus, but you will not always have a Bible available. Make sure you know what the Bible has to say about Jesus and God's gift of salvation.

c. Invitation

Finally, you have the opportunity to invite others to become seekers and followers of Jesus. John the Baptist did that. *"The next day John was there again with two of his disciples. When he saw Jesus passing by, he said, 'Look, the Lamb of God!' When the two disciples heard him say this, they followed Jesus"* (John 1:35-37). Through John's simple invitation, Jesus gained two more followers.

CrossQuote

When some Greeks tried to approach Jesus, Andrew told them how to find Him.
(John 12:20-22

Andrew was an interesting man. We don't read about him preaching mighty sermons, nor do we have scripture penned by Andrew. What made him special was that he was always bringing others to Jesus. The first thing Andrew did after meeting Jesus was go and tell his brother Peter (John 1:41). It was Andrew who spoke to the boy with the loaves and fishes and brought him to Jesus (John 6:8-9). *When some Greeks tried to approach Jesus, Andrew told them how to find Him (John 12:20-22)*. Whereas Andrew's brother Peter was gregarious and outspoken, Andrew often worked behind the scenes. Yet both disciples were effective witnesses for Christ. Andrew is a good role model in witnessing. Look for opportunities on campus and in the community to invite someone to a Christian student meeting or to a service at your church. Give out tracts, Christian books, or CDs to people you know. You will regularly have opportunities in your conversations to invite others to Jesus. You can even tell about Christ in a Chat Room through the Internet. For some students, this is the best way to get their attention. Everyone reads their email.

Reflecting on Our Christian Witness

Sometimes it is difficult to carry our cross before others. We don't necessarily want to attract attention. Yet if we are to be faithful to Christ's command, we must take up our cross and follow Him into any witnessing situation. Take a few minutes to consider the following questions:

1. What can I do as a CrossSeeker to affirm the Gospel message? List one or two ideas in the space below.

2. What can I do as a CrossSeeker to share my faith each time God gives me an opportunity? What are some common ways I can do this on campus? Jot down two or three ideas that you know you can do.

3. Is there someone with whom I should share Christ, but I have not? How can I prepare myself to be ready at the next opportunity to witness? Do I need to take a course that will help me be an effective witness?

Prayer of Commitment (Put in your own words.)

Dear Lord,
Forgive me for when I have been ashamed to carry my cross before others and to share my faith with them. I realize You were not ashamed to claim me as Your disciple. As a CrossSeeker, I never want to be ashamed to claim You as my Savior and Lord. Help me to be sensitive to people You want me to tell of Your love. I commit myself to seize every opportunity to tell others about You. Amen.

Chapter 7

SERVICE
THE ATTITUDE OF THE CROSS: GIVING YOUR LIFE FOR OTHERS

"The Spirit of the Lord is on me, because He has anointed me to preach the good news to the poor. He has sent me to proclaim freedom for the prisoners and recovery of sight for the blind, to release the oppressed, to proclaim the year of the Lord's favor."
Luke 4:18-19

I believe that God desires to draw all people into a loving, redeeming relationship with Him. As His disciple, I will give myself to be His hands to reach others in ministry and missions.

THE ATTITUDE OF THE CROSS:
GIVING YOUR LIFE FOR OTHERS

Norman Schwarzkopf, commander of the Desert Storm operation against Iraq, also fought in the Vietnam War. While there, a company under his command inadvertently walked into a minefield, and several soldiers were injured when a mine exploded. The book *Schwarzkopf in His Own Words* says that when Schwarzkopf arrived on the scene by helicopter, he began assembling the wounded for evacuation. The rest of the men, trapped in the minefield, were on the verge of panic. From the edge of the minefield, Schwarzkopf called out instructions, guiding the men back to safety. Suddenly, a young soldier stepped on another mine. Badly wounded, he was thrashing about in agony and in danger of detonating another mine and killing his companions. Schwarzkopf commanded the wounded man to remain still and then entered the field himself. When he got to the soldier, Schwarzkopf called to four soldiers standing in what appeared to be relative safety at the edge of the minefield to cut branches from a nearby tree for splints. As one soldier moved to respond, he stepped on a mine, and he and two others were killed instantly. Ironically, entering the minefield to save the wounded soldier, instead of staying on the edge of the danger with the other soldiers, had probably saved Schwarzkopf's life.

Jesus said: *"For whoever wants to save his life will lose it, but whoever loses his life for me will find it"* (Matthew 16:25). Only when you follow Christ's example of sacrificial service for others will you truly experience the abundant life Christ has for you.

Focus on the Cross

Jesus' ministry was one of humble service. Paul exhorted Christians by saying:

> *"Your attitude should be the same as that of Christ Jesus: Who, being in very nature God, did not consider equality with God something to be grasped, but made himself nothing, taking the very nature of a servant, being made in human likeness. And being found in appearance as a man, he humbled himself and became obedient to death—even death on a cross!"*
> *(Philippians 2:5-8).*

What an incredible servant's heart! Christ, who was equal with God, did not cling to His rights or status in heaven, but renounced them to assume the role of a servant. Crucifixion was reserved for slaves and the vilest criminals. Jesus humbled Himself so thoroughly that He not only became a man, with every human weakness, but He also suffered man's most ignoble death—that of a slave.

What is your reaction to the thought that you must be like a slave? In the space below, describe your feelings about being a slave.

Jesus displayed this servant attitude when He gathered His disciples for a final meal together before His crucifixion. As each disciple arrived, he noticed there was no servant to wash his feet. Because people wore sandals then, and walked the same paths as animals, all manner of filth accumulated on their feet. Since feet were the dirtiest part of the body, they were considered the most disgraceful. So despicable was the task of washing others' feet that Jewish slaves were exempt from this job. Only foreign slaves were forced to demean themselves in this way. As the disciples entered the room, no one took the humiliating task of washing even his own feet.

Scripture says *"Jesus knew that the Father had put all things under his power, and that he had come from God and was returning to God" (John 13:3)*. Jesus knew who He was. He knew He had authority from His Father, and that He was going to return to the right hand of God. He had nothing to prove. His identity and self-worth were secure.

The same could not be said of the disciples. James may have been thinking, "I'm not going to wash people's feet. I'm the oldest. They should be washing mine." Peter may have thought, "I am the leader of this group. How would it look if I behaved like a servant?" No one wanted to appear less important than the others. Everyone wanted to be served rather than to serve. While each disciple waited to see if someone else would serve them, Jesus took a basin of water and a towel and began, one by one, to wash the disciples' feet. The sound of the water splashing back into the basin as their Teacher scrubbed their dirty feet must have deeply touched the disciples. Even Judas, who would soon betray Jesus, had his feet carefully washed.

When Jesus finished, He said to His disciples, *"I have set you an example that you should do as I have done for you" (John 13:15)*. The mark of a genuine CrossSeeker would be that you will serve others with the same attitude that Christ had demonstrated. As a CrossSeeker, do you wash others' feet through Christian service? (Circle one reflective of your lifestyle at this moment.)

Yes   No   Often   Seldom   Never

Have you seen this attitude in anyone on campus? Describe the situation and why you thought the person was a servant.

Focus on Our Service:
A Visit to the Retirement Home

One day my pastor called and asked if I could lead a worship service at a retirement home in our town. I agreed and prepared a sermon. My wife and I thought this might be an enriching experience for our children, so we went as a family. Trying to preach a sermon that evening was unusually challenging. The residents were polite, and they did not disrupt the service, but I could not establish eye contact. They all stared at my children who were seated at the side of the room. Elderly worshipers sitting close to them reached out to touch them; others waved; others smiled or winked. Realizing they were too distracted to listen to me preach, I ended the service. Those seniors immediately rushed toward my children. Moments later, to my amazement, I noticed a frail, elderly woman pushing my long-legged, ten-year-old son in a metal cart down a long hallway. I shouted, "Mike! Get out of that cart!" I could just imagine this poor woman having a heart attack from the exertion. What would my pastor say?

At the end of the hall the woman turned to me and with a feeble wave of her hand said, "I *asked* him to get in. I'm giving him a ride." Then the woman shuffled slowly all the way back down the long hallway, with my grinning son in her cart. I thought we should go home, but as we were getting our coats on, the woman stopped us and said, "Wait! I have to give the *other* children a ride, too." My wife and I shrugged, smiled, and ushered our next son toward the cart, thankful that he was a little lighter than Mike. We knew we were in for a long evening. When we finally pulled out of the parking lot to go home, our children were bewildered. "Why did that lady do that?" they asked.

"Well," I replied, "you probably won't completely understand this now, but tonight God used you to be a blessing." It had been a simple thing. No big deal. Yet that evening God had used our family, more specifically our children, to bless others. Most of the time, service does not depend on our skills nearly as much as it does our willingness.

As a CrossSeeker, think of a way you can serve other students on your campus. Write it here.

If you are going to serve others effectively, you need to understand some things.

First, you need to know who you are. In western society, we aspire to be CEOs, not servants. Yet as a child of God, you are a fellow heir with Christ. You are dearly loved by Almighty God. Serving others will never diminish your worth in God's eyes.

Second, you need to be aware of God's presence. Jesus always looked to see where His Father was working and then joined Him. As you, too, join God where He is at work, you will never be alone. When you volunteer to teach Sunday School at a small mission church, or serve food to street people, or tutor an international student on Friday evenings, you may think you are serving alone, but God is with you. Times of service can provide you with some of the most precious and intimate times of fellowship with God. He will give you the strength you need, the words to speak, and the love necessary to be His servant as you minister to others in His name. Knowing God is with you frees you from the need to be thanked and given credit for your acts of service.

Finally, like Jesus, you need to understand your future. Second Corinthians 5:10 says that we must all stand before the judgment seat of Christ to account for our actions. Knowing this, we serve even when it is difficult, because we know that one day we will give an account for our actions to the greatest Servant.

Following are *some ways* a CrossSeeker can serve others:

1. Giving Your Time

Students are busy people, no question. Even so, you probably have more time than money to give to others. It takes creativity to know how best to invest time in others. A singles group I was in "adopted" a local orphanage and went there each month just to spend time with the kids. Other students volunteered to serve food at homeless shelters. Others offered to rake leaves, mow lawns, and shovel snow for the elderly. Students have given time to be "big brothers" or "big sisters" to single-parent kids. Some students would spend their Saturday evenings at a youth drop-in center befriending teenagers who had no one to talk to.

> **CrossQuote**
>
> *They appreciate the time he spent being a friend when they needed one.*

As a college student, my brother, Tom, spent time with boys who did not have fathers living at home. He taught one boy how to play the trumpet, another to swim, and another to play racquetball. Tom has continued this practice over the years. I am never surprised when a young boy approaches me and shyly asks me if I am related to Tom. There are young men all over the world who still write to him and call him. *They appreciate the time he spent being a friend when they needed one.* Time is precious, and if invested wisely, can make a tremendous difference in others' lives.

2. Loving the Unlovable

I remember receiving a phone call from Wayne, a fellow student, one evening. Through his tears he described how he and his father had become embroiled in another bitter argument. His father became so furious he threw his son out the back door and ordered him never to return. Wayne had nowhere to live. He had not experienced much love from his father while growing up. His father had been a poor role model, so Wayne had a lot of rough edges. There were times he would say foolish things or show little tact. He could be pushy and manipulative, yet he desperately needed to experience persistent love. He stayed with me in my room at home for the next couple of nights while I helped him find a place to live. Three college students offered to let him live with them in the house they were renting. Other students encouraged him, while others invited him for meals.

My student group tended to attract people who desperately needed to be loved. There was Peter, who was a chronic liar and a thief. We invited him to play on our hockey team, but he used the opportunity to steal our watches and cash from the dressing room during the game. We had Ken, who tried to impress the girls by bragging about how many days he had gone without brushing his teeth! We had a single-parent student who monopolized each Bible study complaining about her problems. There were those who had been sexually abused who struggled with relationships. There were the perennial students who never wanted to graduate, fearing what lay beyond school. There was Dan, who was expelled from the school's athletic program because of a violent outburst during a league game. There were lonely students who drifted from group to group trying to find a place they could fit in. All of these needed someone who would love them unconditionally and not turn them away because of their problems.

Which kinds of people do you feel comfortable ministering to? (Check all that apply.)

❑ Internationals   ❑ wealthy   ❑ unattractive

❑ outspoken   ❑ sensitive   ❑ Christlike

❑ sexually abused   ❑ unhappy   ❑ mentally challenged

❑ average   ❑ smart   ❑ physically challenged

❑ young   ❑ old   ❑ dirty

How difficult was it for Jesus to wash the feet of Judas who would soon run to betray Him? Knowing that Peter would deny Him or that the others would desert Him did not stop Jesus from ministering to them, for Jesus' service to others was not based on what they deserved or on how they treated Him, but on what His Father asked Him to do.

Likewise, we love others as an act of obedience, not as a response to how loveable they are. When God brings people our way who are hard to love, He is stretching us in the area of obedience. As we love them, our capacity for love increases.

3. Sharing Your Resources

As a student, you may feel you are barely getting by. Yet you probably have more than you realize. Your vehicle might not be much, but it can be a great help to others. I had a sorry excuse for a car while I was a student. It was so dilapidated that my father-in-law would only agree to let me marry his daughter if I promised to sell my car and keep hers. My jalopy was a constant target for teasing as well as for toilet paper vandals! When the motor vehicle licensing agency filled in the color on the registration form, they simply put "rust." Yet it was a blessing to me and to others. Every Sunday I picked up an elderly widow from the senior citizen's home and took her to church. Her eyesight had deteriorated, so she rode proudly along with me! Your dorm or room at home can also be valuable for service. Just having the willingness to share your home, no matter how plain or how small, can make it a hub of Christian activity for your campus.

If you were to talk to your director of student ministry, huddle coach, or other Christian leader on campus and offer "resources," what are some of the things you could offer? Write them here.

1.   5.

2.   6.

3.   7.

4.   8.

4. Serving in the Church

The local church provides numerous opportunities for students to serve others. While she was a college student, my wife, Lisa, offered to teach children's Sunday School at a mission church in a little prairie town called Allan. There were few teachers and lots of children, so her class had a wide age range. When she arrived one Sunday, the room was filled with unruly kids of all ages, and she felt overwhelmed. Having received no training for teaching such a diverse group, she did the best she could. The children were unusually hyper on this particular Sunday, and three-quarters of the way through the class, Lisa had had enough. She bolted for her car in tears and raced 40 miles back to her home without telling anyone she had left! After talking with her pastor, she felt ready to try again. She returned to her class the next week, and over the next two years she became their beloved teacher.

As a college student, I agreed to serve as the chairman of the ushers for my church. We had a problem with one young boy. He would wait until the pastor began his message, then he would get up and stomp through the auditorium en route to the rest room. I enlisted a fellow student, a star football player, as an usher and told him about our predicament. The next Sunday, the boy with the heavy feet began his ritual of noisily exiting during the sermon. Halfway down the aisle he spotted the new and very eager linebacker/usher waiting for him at the back of the church, hands on hips. The boy stopped dead in his tracks, spun around, and tiptoed back to his seat. Problem solved!

As a CrossSeeker involved in a New Testament church, maybe no committee has contacted you about serving in some capacity. If you were to go to them and explain some of what you enjoy doing to help others, what would you offer? List three things you can offer.

1.

2.

3.

Now, go to the pastor or some leader of the church and offer these acts of service, willingly and with humility to the church.

Monuments of Service

During the 19th century, the Loretto Chapel was built in Santa Fe, New Mexico. As the modest chapel neared completion, a problem became evident. The chapel was small and could not accommodate many people. The choir loft was located in a balcony to the rear of the chapel. In order to build a staircase for the choir to use to get to the balcony, many pews would have to be removed from the main floor, greatly reducing the number of available seats. Instead, the church placed a ladder by the balcony so each choir member could ascend to the choir loft. Most of the men had no difficulty, but the nuns in their cumbersome garments struggled with this procedure. The congregation began praying that God would send someone who could help them solve their dilemma.

One day in 1878, a mysterious peasant arrived at the chapel. He had brought some simple carpentry tools with him. He set to work building a peculiar staircase. Unlike normal staircases which gradually ascend in a horizontal direction, his staircase rose straight up to the balcony in a spiral. It was an engineering marvel because there were no supports to hold up the weight of the staircase. It appeared to simply rise straight up to the balcony, suspended in air. Once the peasant carpenter had finished, he disappeared without seeking payment and was never heard from again. For over a hundred years, choirs ascended and descended the staircase as they sang to worship God. To this day, the staircase stands as a monument to the glory of God and to a humble carpenter who gave his skills in service to the church.

Your service as a CrossSeeker and a Christian is your monument to glorify God. As you use the skills and possessions God has given you for His glory in His church, His people will be strengthened. When God gives you something, He expects you to share it with others. It might be that God has blessed you with computer skills. Sharing your knowledge of computers with others or with your church can be a unique expression of Christian service. Perhaps you could tutor a struggling student in a subject in which you excel, or help a foreign student practice speaking English. You can help a new student move into an apartment. Do you have mechanical ability? Why not repair the vehicle of a single mother who cannot afford to pay for repairs? Your architectural training could be used to design renovations for your church building. It may be that your accounting skills are desperately needed by your church finance committee. You may be a graphic arts student who can design brochures and advertisements for your church. If you are a music student, share your talents in the worship services at your church. God has gifted you in some way. Your responsibility is to share that gift with those around you through service. You might consider finding a small mission church where your life can have a greater impact and offering them your services.

My student group had a large number of medical and nursing students who regularly attended the Wednesday evening prayer services at our church. One Wednesday evening, a woman fainted. So many students rushed to her aid that the auditorium looked like a hospital emergency ward. The few of us remaining in our seats with no medical training watched in amusement as these eager students practiced their new skills on the unsuspecting woman!

Reflecting on Our Service
As a CrossSeeker, serving others with your time, resources, and abilities can be difficult, especially if you feel you are unappreciated or downright unloved by them. Service requires that you deny your own comfort and allow Christ to minister to someone else through you.

Self Check
1. After reading this chapter, am I comfortable being a servant? Why or why not?

2. Covenant living calls for me to be a servant. How am I presently serving others?

3. Thinking of those around me, whose life can I help make better because of my service?

4. What are three things I could do this week to serve others? List them!

1.

2.

3.

Prayer of Commitment (Put it in your own words.)

Dear Lord,
*Forgive me for wanting to be served instead of seeking to serve others. Help me be a CrossSeeker committed to seeking opportunities to serve in Christ's name. Please remove the selfishness in me that wants to receive Your blessings without sharing them with others. Make me aware of those around me whom I can help. I **commit myself** to find creative, practical, and meaningful ways to serve others and to begin doing so today. Amen.*

Chapter 8

PURITY

PURIFIED BY THE CROSS

"Do you not know that your body is a temple of the Holy Spirit, who is in you, whom you have received from God? You are not your own; you were bought at a price. Therefore honor God with your body."
I Corinthians 6:19-20

Following the example of Christ, I will keep my body healthy and strong, avoiding temptations and destructive personal vices. I will honor the gift of life by keeping myself sexually pure and free from addictive drugs.

In the News: Isn't it Obvious?

Many things once thought obvious are no longer assumed so by manufacturers. As stated in a news account, one bottle of flavored milk cautions: "After opening, keep upright." A package of peanuts warns: "Contains nuts." An airline serves packages of nuts with the message: "Instructions: Open packet, eat contents." A Swedish chain saw manufacturer advises: "Do not try to stop chain with hands." Marks & Spencer stores have a warning on their pudding packages: "Product will be hot after heating." An electrical manufacturer gives the sage warning: "Do not iron clothes on body." A camera had the disclaimer: "This camera only works when there is film inside."

These instructions are so obvious they seem ridiculous to print, yet every year people suffer harm or difficulties due to their own igno-rance. The result is the birth of a lucrative litigation industry. People bring lawsuits against manufacturers they believe did not adequately warn them about potential dangers. For example, you would assume a person who is highly allergic to nuts would know to avoid eating a bag of peanuts. Yet, unless the bag carries the warning, "Contains nuts," there are those who would feel entitled to compensation after suffer-ing ill effects from eating them.

Just as these manufacturers are issuing warnings concerning the obvious, God has always made it clear that violating His spiritual laws would inevitably lead to our destruction. Because God has been straightforward about the results of our sin, CrossSeekers and other Christians have no one to blame but ourselves when we suffer the inevitable consequences.

It seems logical that feeding a mind with immorality would lead to an immoral lifestyle. One might assume if you abused your body with drugs, a high-fat diet, a lack of exercise, or smoking, it would suffer ill effects. Yet millions of people abuse their minds and bodies and then complain about a loving God who allows them to suffer.

Focus on the Cross

The fundamental message of the cross is found in 1 Peter 2:24:
"He himself bore our sins in his body on the tree, so that we might die to sins and live for righteousness; by his wounds you have been healed."

The cross is where God dealt decisively with our sin. Mankind was hopelessly enslaved to evil (John 8:34). Despite our most noble and strenuous efforts, we could not stop sinning or become holy enough to satisfy God's righteousness. So God sent His only Son to pay the penalty for our sin. *Every sin we will ever commit was charged to His account, and He was put to death to pay for it.* By *His* wounds, *we* found healing. And since we have been liberated from our oppressive sin, we are now free as CrossSeekers to live in purity as God desires.

CrossQuote

Every sin we will ever commit was charged to His account, and He was put to death to pay for it.

The Apostle Peter charged: *"But just as he who calls you is holy, so be holy in all you do" (1 Peter 1:15).* Because we have been called by holy God, we are obligated to live holy lives. To be holy means to be absolutely pure, without moral blemish. It means we are different from the world—we are like God. Peter also urged us to *"make every effort to be found spotless, blameless and at peace with him" (2 Peter 3:14).* The desire to be holy is not enough. Nor is it sufficient to acknowledge that holiness is a worthy goal. God expects CrossSeekers and all Christians to *make every effort* to be spotless and blameless in our relationship with Him and with others. Everything is in place for us to live a life of purity. It is up to us to decide whether or not we will do so.

List some examples of moral blemishes on society today.

What groups or organizations are seeking to combat the "blemishes" on your campus? In your community?

In The News: A Second Chance to Live

Private Henry Tandey was serving in the Duke of Wellington's regiment on September 28, 1918, when his exploits won him Britain's highest military honor: the Victoria Cross. It was World War I, and Tandey's regiment was active at Marcoing, France in hand-to-hand combat. As Tandey was fighting fiercely in the battle where he won his medal, he came upon a wounded German corporal. Tandey aimed his rifle at the helpless German, as he had so many other times that day, but this time he felt compassion for the defenseless soldier. He lowered his rifle and turned away. After World War I, the German soldier entered politics but never forgot the mercy shown him by Tandey. In 1933, he sent investigators to the British military museums and discovered Tandey's identity. He then ordered a print of a painting of Tandey and hung it in his home. Later, while entertaining the British prime minister, the German pointed out Tandey's portrait on the wall and said, "That man came so close to killing me. I thought I would never see Germany again." The German had received a second chance at life. When his life seemed to be at its end, he received mercy and a new opportunity to make a contribution to humanity. Unfortunately, the German chose a different path for his life. Rather than using his new lease on life for good, he chose to provoke the most brutal war in history. The German soldier's name, according to the *Calgary Herald*, was Adolph Hitler.

If you had received mercy the way Hitler did, how do you think that might have affected the way you lived the rest of your life? Write one or two ideas here.

Focus on Our Holiness

God's command is clear: *"Be holy because I, the Lord your God, am holy" (Leviticus 19:2).* Every aspect of life as a CrossSeeker or as a Christian: our thoughts, our actions, our body, our lifestyle, and our reputation ought to be dedicated to bringing glory to God. In each of these areas, we need to ask ourselves: "Have I allowed God to remove every sin in this part of my life and to bring purity and holiness in its place?" and, "Having been saved from my sin, am I choosing to allow it into my life anyway?"

1. Purity of Mind

Our thoughts determine our actions. If we are to live holy lives, we must have pure minds. Philippians 4:8 urges: *"Whatever is true, whatever is noble, whatever is right, whatever is pure, whatever is lovely, whatever is admirable—if anything is excellent or praiseworthy—think about such things."* We need to regularly place our thoughts, the books

CrossQuote

We need to regularly place our thoughts, the books we read, the movies we watch, the music we listen to, and the conversations we have before this standard.

we read, the movies we watch, the music we listen to, and the conversations we have before this standard. Too often we excuse what we allow into our minds by comparing it to things that are worse. For example, "I may watch movies with graphic violence and profanity, but at least I don't watch pornography." When you are considering exposing your mind to something questionable, ask yourself: "Is it pure? lovely? right? admirable? of good reputation? noble?" If the answer is "no," then don't do it.

Revival in 1995

During 1995, a revival swept across college campuses in the United States. It began when two students came under profound conviction for the sinfulness of their lives. They felt compelled to confess their sin before fellow students and to be restored in their relationship with God. As they did so, other students realized that they, too, had lives filled with sin. One by one, students publicly confessed the ugliness hidden in their hearts and minds. This movement spread to other campuses as well. Chapel services lasted many hours. Services held in the evening would go into the early morning hours. The services did not consist of preaching, but of students confessing their sin.

The most common confessions were sins of the mind, such as bitterness, lust, anger, jealousy, pride, cheating, racial prejudice, hatred, cynicism, materialism, and competitiveness. An alarming number of male students repented of involvement in pornography. Female students admitted they had been dressing and behaving suggestively in order to promote immoral thoughts among the male students. In one college service, five garbage bags were filled with pornographic books and magazines, inappropriate CD's, drugs, and alcohol that had been collected from repentant students.

It became apparent that students had allowed their minds to be filled with immoral thoughts, and these thoughts were dramatically affecting their lifestyle. When God's holy presence suddenly filled the chapel meetings, the ugliness of the students' thoughts was exposed for what it was, and students repented for hours. (To learn more about this student revival, read the book *Revival!: Brownwood, Ft. Worth, Wheaton, and beyond* by John Avant, Malcolm McDow, and Alvin Reid.)

2. A Sanctified Body

As CrossSeekers, we are responsible not only to glorify God with our thoughts, but also with our bodies. Paul said: *"I urge you, brothers, in view of God's mercy, to offer your bodies as living sacrifices, holy and*

pleasing to God—this is your spiritual act of worship" (Romans 12:1).
At times it may seem easier to die for Christ than to live for Him!
Presenting our bodies daily as a *living* sacrifice means we must regular-
ly overcome the temptation to abuse or neglect them.

Our bodies are also described as God's temple (1 Corinthians 3:16).
God's Holy Spirit dwells within us. The Israelites had to carefully maintain the temple in order to honor God; so, too, we must each honor
God by the way we care for the body He has given us. What are some
ways we can honor our bodies as temples of God? Write out a word or
sentence on each line to describe a positive thing you can do:

Exercise_____

Eating habits_____

Weight_____

Stress_____

Relaxation_____

Meditation _____

Sleep_____

Drug Use_____

Study/Work_____

A Home or a Jungle?

I am highly allergic to cats. One day I travelled to a distant city to
preach in the church of a friend. The pastor, a wonderful Christian
man, graciously invited me to stay in his home. When I got to his
house, I telephoned my wife, Lisa, to let her know I had arrived safely.
As we talked, Lisa asked, "Are there cats in that house?"

"I don't know. Why do you ask?" I replied.

"Because you sound like you always do when you have an allergic
reaction to cats."

Suddenly I felt something brush against my ankle. I looked down to see the fuzzy family cat at my feet. Then a shaggy dog ran into the room, furiously wagging its tail. I had already counted three turtles in a tank by the television. Then one child came in with a bird; another with a hamster. Just when I thought I had detoured through a pet store, the pastor entered the room with a boa constrictor coiled around his throat! He told me one of his sons had offered his bedroom for the night. Muffling the first of many sneezes, I feebly thanked him. He replied cheerily, "No problem! As long as you don't mind bunking with the cat and the snake."

This was a wonderful family, and they were gracious hosts. But there were some things in their house that made me extremely uncomfortable! Likewise, if we allow harmful things into our bodies, we cannot expect to honor the Holy Spirit who resides within us. It will be difficult to tell others about the victory Christ can give them if our bodies demonstrate that we are experiencing defeat in our eating habits. Paul said our bodies were no longer our own. They exist to bring glory to God. When we overeat and become overweight, when we intoxicate ourselves with alcohol and dull our minds, when we take drugs and become addicted to destructive chemicals, when we smoke tobacco and fill our lungs with carcinogens, we are not bringing glory to God. When we engage in sexual activity outside of marriage, we expose our bodies to disease and even death. When we don't exercise or get enough rest, we abuse the very bodies we are to give to God as a sacrifice. When we gamble, we give up the control of our minds for the sake of pleasure and entertainment.

Sometime this week, share your concern about Christian purity with other like-minded Christian students on campus. Develop strategies which would allow you to share the good news of purity with non-believers.

In Old Testament times, God demanded His people sacrifice to Him the best animals they had as an expression of their love and worship. God demanded the animals be without defect or blemish. People offered God their best to demonstrate that God was worthy of everything they had. In the same way, when God commands us to offer our bodies as a sacrifice, we are obligated to present them in the best condition we possibly can. To carelessly abuse our bodies and then offer them to God is an insult. God expects our best in everything we do, including the way we take care of what He has given us.

3. A Sanctified Lifestyle

Will Rogers, the popular comedian, said, "So live that you wouldn't mind selling the family parrot to the town gossip." As CrossSeekers and Christians, we are obligated to live above reproach. Peter urged: *"Make every effort to be found spotless, blameless and at peace with him" (1 Peter 3:14).* Being blameless means there is no activity or habit in our lives that is morally questionable. There is nothing in our lifestyle that would offend or cause weaker Christians to stumble in their relationships with Christ. There is nothing we are doing that would bring shame to the name of Christ.

In The News: Blowing the Whistle

The Center for Disease Control and Prevention claims that dirty hands are a growing national health risk, according to a recent newspaper account. More than 40 million Americans get sick with diseases such as hepatitis, and approximately 80,000 die each year from hand- and air-borne bacteria. Despite the obvious health risk of dirty hands, University of Iowa Hospital researchers discovered that only three out of five health care workers in the intensive care unit washed their hands before tending to their patients. The American Society for Microbiology found that just 60 percent of those using rest rooms in New York City's Penn Station washed their hands. In an effort to encourage people to do so, technology is being implemented in various hospitals, restaurants, and businesses. Employees are given special tags to wear, and infrared sensors detect when they enter a rest room. An alarm will sound if that person does not spend at least 15 seconds in front of the sink, presumably to wash his or her hands. People somehow believe they can expose themselves to all kinds of germs and yet remain unaffected. This attitude is spreading sickness and death all over the country.

Likewise, as CrossSeekers and Christians, we sometimes think we can expose ourselves to sinful thoughts, relationships, practices, and lifestyles and not have these affect our relationships with God or with others. A married man regularly lunches alone with a married woman and claims his actions are innocent and will not affect his spiritual life or harm his marriage. A student cheats on exams and takes shortcuts with hisstudies, but maintains that it will not affect the way he relates to people or his future job performance. We need to examine every activity in light of the end result, asking the question: "Does this behavior reflect the actions of someone seeking to be found *spotless* and blameless before God?" Our infrared sensor is the Holy Spirit living within us. His role is to alert and convict us every time we begin to stray from God's standard. Christians have to actively resist the pleadings of the Holy Spirit in order to continue in habitual sin (1 Thessalonians 5:19-22).

Scripture indicates we will never face a temptation that is beyond our ability to resist. First Corinthians 10:13 promises: *"No temptation has seized you except what is common to man. And God is faithful; he will not let you be tempted beyond what you can bear. But when you are tempted, he will also provide a way out so that you can stand up under it."* The Bible promises that there is always an escape from temptation. The problem with many people who are tempted is that they flee, but they leave a forwarding address! They know they have a weakness for alcohol, or pornography, or gossip, or adultery, or dishonesty, yet they continually put themselves in a position where they will be tempted once again. The Bible's common-sense solution to temptation is: Flee! Don't remain in the midst of temptation hoping for a victory. Get away from it!

CrossQuote

Likewise, as CrossSeekers and Christians, we sometimes think we can expose ourselves to sinful thoughts, relationships, practices and lifestyles and not have these affect our relationship with God or others.

In The News: Don't Take Pictures!

In the Rocky Mountains near where I live, people are mauled by grizzly bears almost every year. Even though people are warned of the danger, hikers, hunters, and tourists regularly travel into the areas where bears have been spotted. Last summer, a local paper told this story: Four hikers were exploring a mountain trail when they suddenly came upon a hungry grizzly eating berries. The startled bear reared up on its hind legs and growled at the intruders. In response, the hikers did not run away, or hide, or climb a tree, or call for help. They pulled out a video camera and took three minutes of live footage until the bear finally charged them!

Even more foolish are those who toy with temptation, assuming they will not be hurt. When temptation comes, as it surely will, they would do well to listen to the Holy Spirit's warnings and the pleading of concerned Christian friends, and remove themselves from that which can destroy them.

Reflecting on the Cross and Our Holiness

God is clear about His expectations: "Be holy!" What is not so clear is what our response will be when we face temptation. Sometimes we struggle with moral temptations. Other times physical sins entice us. Whatever temptations we encounter, however, we know God can give us victory over them.

Self Check

1. What are some lifestyle changes you could make that would bring greater glory to God?

2. Do you have a reputation with God and with people for being holy?

Prayer of Commitment

Dear Lord,
*Forgive me for the times I have run toward temptation rather than flee from it. Forgive me for making excuses and trying to justify my unholy living rather than striving to be holy in everything I do. Create in me a hatred for sin in my life and sensitize my heart to Your Holy Spirit's voice, so that when He warns me of temptation, I will heed His voice immediately. Because of Your mercy, grace, and strength, **I commit myself** to live from this day forward with a mind, body, and lifestyle that are holy before You. Amen.*

CHRISTLIKE RELATIONSHIPS

RELATIONSHIPS: TRANSFORMED BY THE CROSS

"Therefore, as God's chosen people, holy and dearly loved, clothe yourselves with compassion, kindness, humility, gentleness, and patience. Bear with each other and forgive what grievances you may have with one another. Forgive as the Lord forgave you. And over all these virtues put on love, which binds them all together in perfect unity."
Colossians 3:12-14

In every relationship and in every situation, I will seek to live as Christ would. I will work to heal brokenness, to value each person as a child of God, to avoid petty quarrels and harsh words, to let go of bitterness and resentment that hinder genuine Christian love.

CHAPTER 9

Jim and Christine lived an idyllic small town romance. They met in high school and soon became best friends. She was an ice skater, pretty, athletic, and full of life. He was an outdoors enthusiast. After dating for four years, they were married, and Jim went to work for his father-in-law. Jim and Christine dreamed of buying a home, raising a family, and living near their parents. It seemed like a fairy tale in the making, but before their first anniversary, disaster struck. Christine suffered a seizure in the middle of the night. Doctors, fearing the worst, sent her to the city for tests. The diagnosis was heart-wrenching: a malignant brain tumor. Surgery revealed the tumor was inoperable. They were devastated. Christine's prognosis was grim—they gave her six months to two years to live. She was only 21.

Aggressive radiation and chemotherapy coupled with heavy doses of drugs resulted in a remission which, amazingly, has lasted almost 20 years. But those years have been far from idyllic for Jim and Christine. Countless trips to the city for tests and medical procedures have eroded their family life and bank account. Christine's mind and body have been radically altered because of the many side effects of powerful medication. She cannot hold a job or drive a car. She requires home care assistance. Weakened by her condition and medication, Christine has never been able to do simple household chores most of us take for granted. Plagued by chronic illness, Christine has been a regular patient at the local hospital.

Jim never could have dreamed this would be the way his life would go the day he stood at the altar with his pretty bride and promised, "In sickness and in health. . . ." As young people, he and Christine never questioned their good health. Now health concerns are a part of their daily lives. Jim has devoted the best years of his life to care for his wife, giving up relationships with his friends, hunting trips, ball games, and other social activities. He has poured all his extra money into health care, prescriptions, and take-out food because of his wife's condition. Jim's married life will never fulfill the potential that he once envisioned. Does Jim ever doubt whether the commitment he made to his wife on their wedding day is binding for life? If he does, it doesn't show. Jim is my brother-in-law, and he continues, year after year, to love, cherish, and honor his wife.

What qualities relating to developing a Christlike relationship do you see in the relationship between Jim and Christine? List at least three.

1.

2

3.

If you were to take the qualities you have listed and develop them into your life as a CrossSeeker, what difference do you think they would make on the relationships you form?

Relationships are not always easy. They can bring the greatest joys as well as the deepest sorrows. Much of the grief associated with relationships comes from broken commitments.

Focus on the Cross

Jesus developed rich and meaningful friendships. His entire ministry on earth was spent establishing relationships with people. This was vividly demonstrated in the hours surrounding His crucifixion.

Knowing He was soon to be arrested and crucified, Jesus chose to spend His final hours with His closest friends, not healing the sick or preaching to the multitudes. Even though He knew one would betray Him and all would forsake Him, *"He loved them to the end" (John 13:1 NASB)*. During the Last Supper, Jesus gave His standard for friendship when He said, *"Greater love has no one than this, that he lay down his life for his friends" (John 15:13)*. Shortly thereafter, Jesus would willingly surrender Himself to be cruelly executed, so He could save His friends. The disciples learned Jesus is a faithful friend for life.

While hanging on the cross, though He was in agony, Jesus continued to demonstrate concern for others. People laughed and mocked Him as He suffered for them. He responded by asking His Father to forgive their sins (Luke 23:34-37). He turned to the thief who had been one of His mockers only minutes earlier and helped him find forgiveness and eternal life (Luke 23:43). Even in Jesus' weakest moments, He demonstrated love for His enemies.

There were others at the cross with Jesus. Mary, His mother, was there along with Mary Magdalene and others who had received

CrossQuote

Despite His excruciating pain, Jesus still sought to make provision for His mother.

forgiveness from Jesus. His friend John was there at the cross, too (John 19:25-27). It was the responsibility of the oldest son to care for a widowed mother. *Despite His excruciating pain, Jesus still sought to make provision for His mother.* Even though each breath brought greater anguish, He caringly assigned His mother's care to His close friend John (John 19:26).

When Paul wanted to describe the kind of care a husband should have for his wife, he thought of Jesus on the cross. Paul exhorted: *"Husbands, love your wives, just as Christ loved the church and gave himself up for her" (Ephesians 5:25).* This is the standard the cross sets for relationships. It is a high standard and one CrossSeekers will never achieve apart from the work of the Holy Spirit in our lives.

Would this high standard for relationships apply to a Christian dating relationship? A friendship? How we treat our family members?

Focus on Our Relationships
Loving Our Family

One of sin's first casualties was the destruction of family relationships. Adam and Eve sinned, and by the next generation there was already a murder in the family. Once sin began its devastating work upon families, immeasurable suffering resulted. The only solution to the pain and brokenness in families is Christ's sacrifice on the cross. The fundamental problem with families today is not economic, social, or political—it is spiritual. Apart from the salvation found in Christ, families will only accelerate their destructiveness.

Do you agree with this last statement? (Check one.)

❑ Yes ❑ No ❑ Sometimes ❑ Never

In The News: Anger at Home

James Shivers was an angry man. A recent news article stated that he was upset about the breakup of his marriage. He was irritated at having to live in his 26-year-old son's apartment for the past six months. And to make matters worse, his son Tony intentionally blocked his view of the college football game on television one afternoon.

Shivers took out his handgun and fired it in Tony's direction. His son grabbed the pistol and beat his father with it. Breaking free, Shivers ran for his shotgun and fired two rounds into his son, killing him.

How could any father become so disoriented in his values he would kill his son in order to get a better look at a football game? Can you identify two reasons this might have happened to James Shivers?

1.

2.

The problem is not poverty; the answer is not money. The problem is not political; the answer is not a new government initiative. The primary problem is not ignorance; the answer is not improved education. The problem is sin. Since mankind's first transgression, sin has been the relentless enemy of family relationships. Only Christ can defeat the sin that destroys families.

Many students grow up in abusive, loveless homes, and as adults they are bitter about their childhood pain. It is not uncommon for them to leave home for college and vow never to return. Year by year they drift further away from their families. Christ came to bring healing and forgiveness to families suffering such pain. Do you know someone from this type background? Can you share Christ's love with this person?

Maybe your parents were the victims of rampant sin in their homes as they were growing up. Maybe they were raised in an environment of selfishness and anger and became wounded adults and wounded parents as a result. Maybe Christ wants you to be the one to forgive past offenses, breaking the old cycle, and beginning a new pattern of healthy Christian homes. If this is the case of a friend of yours, be a listener and encourager, just as Christ would be for you as a CrossSeeker.

Loving Our Friends

Sin has a way of contaminating and destroying friendships. Sin causes us to be selfish; selfishness erodes relationships. Friendship is based on give and take, not just take. Even as Jesus was preparing to face the most terrifying night of His life, He took time to care for His friends (John 13:1-20). Jesus' friendships were such that He always gave far more than He received. He was never too busy to meet the needs of His friends. That is the model He left for His followers as they cultivate friendships with others; our focus should be on what we can do for our friends, rather than on what they can do for us.

In The News: Stealing from Friends

The world of professional hockey was appalled at the disgraceful downfall of Alan Eagleson. A supposed friend to many of hockey's greatest players, he admitted to stealing from those who had trusted him. Eagleson had been the agent and later the players' representative for the National Hockey League. Many considered him their close friend. During a historic series between the NHL and the Soviet Union in 1972, players came to his aid when Soviet soldiers attempted to arrest him. Players respected Eagleson so much they played hockey when injured and received little compensation for their efforts. Some players loyally defended Eagleson at his embezzlement trial, arguing, "I am very proud to be a friend of Alan Eagleson," and, "I've known Al to be very loyal to his friends and supporters." Yet as Eagleson's trial unfolded, it became obvious his prevailing motive in his friendships had been selfishness. He cared only about how his friends could make him money. He shamelessly embezzled from those who trusted him. He pressured players to play when they were injured, endangering their careers in order to accomplish his goals. It was a criminally selfish approach to friendship, and the court sent him to jail for eighteen months as a result.[1]

What do you think drove Eagleson to steal from his friends? Write your answer(s) in the space below.

One of the most troubling examinations you can ever make is to evaluate what kind of friend you have been to others. Ask yourself: Are people happy to have me around? Are people better off personally because I am their friend? Can they trust me?

How do you think your friends would rate you in your relationships? Would they see you to be loving, caring, and Christlike? Place a mark somewhere between "Christlike" and "Not Christlike," reflecting how you feel your friends perceive your relationships.

Christlike_____Not Christlike

If your mark is close to "Christlike," you are well on your way to becoming a CrossSeeker in word and deed.

With the invention of call display telephones, one can know who is calling before answering the phone. When a call comes at mealtime, it is often a telemarketer wanting to clean the furnace, or carpets, or windows, or all three! At other times the call can be from a "taker," someone who only calls to ask for things. I have name display on my phone. At times the name of the caller alerts me that I am about to be asked to do something. When I see certain names on my display, I immediately know they are not calling to find out how they can serve, but how they can *be* served. Some callers only want an audience who will listen to their complaints. One day I suddenly had a troublesome thought: What do people think when they see my name on their call display? Do they immediately think, "Oh good, it's Richard!" Or, do they think, "Oh no! Richard is calling! I wonder what he wants *this* time?" The thought was a reminder to me that I should seek to serve rather than to be served. As CrossSeekers, our relationships with those around us, and even family perhaps far away, are important in our journey.

Jesus knew how to be a friend. Whenever people encountered Jesus, they always received more than they expected. That's why there were crowds following Him wherever He went. When a person complains that they have no friends, I suspect that says more about them than it does about those around them. *Someone who genuinely knows how to be a friend is irresistible.*

CrossQuote

Someone who genuinely knows how to be a friend is irresistible.

Loving Our Enemies

Many of the religious leaders in Jesus' day hated Him because He exposed their hypocrisy. They felt threatened, and they desperately wanted Jesus killed. When they managed to bribe Judas to betray Him and they pressured Pilate to condemn Him, they thought they had won. Amazingly, as Jesus hung on the cross and looked at the sneering, vengeful, murderous men who had put Him there, He forgave them. It was a powerful moment when Jesus looked upon His murderers and prayed, "Father, *forgive* them." Jesus beautifully demonstrated the contrast between God's response to His enemies and the world's. The world says: Don't let people take advantage of . . . . Don't let him get away with . . . . You cannot forgive someone who has done . . . . Forgiveness just lets them get away with . . . . Jesus said to turn the other cheek, walk an extra mile, and respond to evil with good (Matthew 5:38-47).

One of the most difficult human relationships is with one's enemy. Your enemy may be someone you formerly trusted as a friend. It may be your father, your sister, or your boss. It can be anyone who has harmed you or threatens you in some way. As you respond to those who hurt you, Satan will seek to convince you that you cannot and should not forgive them. Jesus says you cannot follow Him unless you forgive. There are no valid excuses for unforgiveness from one seeking the cross. If you are struggling to forgive someone, return to the cross. Witness Jesus dying an excruciating death for murderers, hypocrites, and His most ruthless enemies. Then ask Him for permission to hold a grudge. See if He will make an exception in your case. You know He will not.

In The News: An Enemy Heart

During the Palestinian uprising against Israel in the 1980s, hatred between the two nations was intense. While on a routine patrol, 40-year-old Sgt. Zeev Traum and a fellow soldier were ambushed. Palestinian guerrillas fired 28 rounds into their patrol jeep, killing both men. When Traum's wife and four children were notified of his death, they also received a request. A patient in a local hospital named Hanna Khader was in need of a heart transplant. He would die without the gift of Sgt. Traum's heart. He was a Palestinian. Palestinians had just killed her husband and the father of her four children; now Mrs. Traum had to decide whether to donate her deceased husband's heart to save a Palestinian's life. Life seldom affords opportunities for such swift revenge. But she did not let bitterness dictate her response. The heart of an Israeli was placed into the chest of a Palestinian, and it gave him life.[2]

God asks us to respond to *our* enemies this way. He also changes our hearts so we are capable of loving those who have hurt us. As a CrossSeeker, have you found it hard to forgive your enemies? Now you know the way Christ would have you relate. Did Mrs. Traum do the right thing? Why? Why not?

Loving Our Spouse

Though Jesus was never married, His model of love became the standard for Christian marriages. You may not be married. But many students meet their spouse on the college campus. For the CrossSeeker, Ephesians 5:25 indicates that as Christ loved the church and laid down His life for her on the cross, husbands are to do the same for their wives. Relationships between men and women are not based on what each can receive, but on what each can give. Marriage is not a 50/50 relationship with each party obligated to give an equal amount. It is a commitment to do everything within your power to help your spouse become all that God wants him or her to be. This may mean that you delay your education so that your spouse can finish his degree. It may mean you take on a second job so you can help your spouse finish her education. Laying down your life means that you consistently put the welfare of your spouse before your own desires.

Some students have never learned how to properly treat someone of the opposite sex. If they did not see a healthy marriage modeled by their parents, Hollywood may have formed their view of relationships. There are clues that reveal whether you have gained your approach to relationships from the world or from Christ. If you say things like: "If you really loved me you would . . .," or, "After all I've done for you, you ought to . . .," or, "I won't be happy unless you . . .," then you are not following Christ's example for relationships. If you are considering marriage, ask yourself, "Is this person someone for whom I could lay down my life?" If you don't think so, don't get married. If the one you are dating is selfish and fails to treat you with respect, don't assume that will change once you are married!

She Gave Her Life

Kevin and Dorothy Murphy had been married for 42 years. Kevin, a well-known lawyer, was nearing retirement. Dorothy operated a popular bed and breakfast in the century-old mansion where they had raised their 12 children. One cold winter afternoon, a stack of papers lying near a wood stove ignited, and the blaze quickly engulfed the entire house. Kevin, overcome by smoke, collapsed several yards from the door. Dorothy, still able to flee, refused to leave her husband. Rather, she began dragging him through the house toward the front door. Just six feet from the exit, Dorothy also succumbed to the smoke and fell across her husband. Moments later, firemen discovered the Murphys, but it was too late. Said a long-time friend of the Murphys, "It would be just like her . . . Dorothy would have thought much more about saving Kevin than saving herself." Dorothy proved she had a relationship in which she would readily give her life for her spouse.

It is not easy to go against the philosophy of this age and develop Christlike relationships. Our society leans more toward getting rather than giving. It encourages us into shallow and momentary relationships and asks that we be satisfied with the moment. It takes the work of the Holy Spirit to enable Christians to develop relationships which are at the level God desires.

In The News: Where Are You Looking?

Policemen with cancer sued their departments for compensation. An alarmingly high number of policemen who regularly used the early models of radar guns to catch speeders developed cancer. Officers would rest the device in their laps or on their shoulders while waiting for the next passing car. Later, many would develop cancer in the places on the body most frequently exposed to the radar gun. It seemed that in a real sense, although they pointed their radar guns at someone else in order to find fault, they were literally killing themselves.[3]

Much of the problem with today's relationships is that, like those policemen, we point our radar at others, hoping to expose their faults. However, if we focus on the failures of others, we will never be satisfied in our relationships. Jesus was keenly aware of other people's sin, yet rather than becoming discouraged or critical of others, He gave His life to provide what was lacking. If, rather than pointing our fingers, we will allow God to shape us into the friend, spouse, and family member He wants us to be, our relationships will be radically transformed.

Focus on Our Relationships

Relationships can be extremely rewarding or extremely frustrating, depending on our point of view. It is critical that we view relationships through the perspective of the cross.

Self-Check

1. Do I approach relationships more concerned about what I will *receive* or how I can *give*?

2. Am I a blessing to my family members, or do I cause them pain?

3. Am I the kind of friend who helps others become more Christlike?

4. In my dating relationships, do I lay down my life for others, or do I ask others to lay down their lives for me?

5. Do I truly love my enemies, or are there people I am refusing to forgive?

Prayer of Commitment

Dear Lord,
Forgive me for being selfish in my relationships. I am sorry for refusing to forgive those who have hurt me. I want to be a blessing to others rather than expecting friendships to benefit me. With Your strength, I **commit myself** *to be the family member and friend who relates to others in the same way Christ does. Amen.*

Notes

1. *Maclean's,* January 19, 1998, 22-30.

2. *Winnipeg Free Press,* November 17, 1989, 29.

3. Ibid., October 22, 1991, C-42.

CROSS
SEEKERS™

LEADER HELPS

This section is designed to facilitate small group study. Follow the suggested outline or adapt it as necessary for a meaningful learning experience for both teacher and students.

Read the book carefully. It is intended to introduce the CrossSeekers Covenant. The Covenant is based on a student's desire for a more meaningful and authentic Christian walk. As students make this commitment, perhaps others will begin to see that being a seeker after the cross of Christ is a worthy journey.

The first three chapters provide background information related to what a "covenant" is all about. The first chapter introduces the call to become a CrossSeeker and what is involved. In the second chapter, a scriptural understanding of how God understands the word "covenant" is presented. Chapter three provides a more contemporary version of this word. Contrast the world's understanding of "covenant" against the example of Christ from current news, experiences, and daily examples.

Chapters four through nine give detailed information concerning the biblical basis for each principle of the Covenant. Additional resources to help students adopt the CrossSeekers lifestyle are offered at the end of the book. In addition to the ones listed, more books will be released throughout the year. For current information on what is available, please contact us on the Web at **www.crossseekers.org.** Along with cost items, Bible studies are available free of charge at this site to be downloaded and shared with friends on campus.

Advertise the study of *CrossSeekers: Discipleship Covenant for a New Generation* and the beginning date. Enlist students who are creative and artistic to help with advertising. If you are beginning a CrossSeekers group, clip art for promotion is available at no charge. To request the clip art, contact us by email at www:crossseekers.org. If you do not have access to the Web, please call us at 615-251-2777 for a hard copy of the clip art.

Before beginning the study, order a copy of this book for each participant. Distribute books before the first meeting, if possible. Encourage students to bring their books to each group session along with pencil, paper, and a Bible.

Secure a comfortable and quiet meeting room where students can write easily and talk freely among themselves as the study progresses.

Although overhead cels for presentation are not provided, permission is granted to create these teaching aids.

Pray for an openness among the students as they begin this journey. Remember, for some it will be the beginning of the spiritual journey. For others, it will be a time to reexamine spiritual truths taught to them as children or youth. They are no longer youth. They are young adults claiming a faith of their own. Hopefully, they will desire to be CrossSeekers!

OUTLINE FOR TEACHING

Begin each session with prayer. . .
- for participants.

- for leaders.

- for clarity of thought.

- for others who desire to be CrossSeekers but cannot make a commitment at this time.

- for Scripture to be communicated clearly and without compromise.

- for authentic relationships to be developed and cultivated.

Examine the CrossSeekers Covenant before each study.

Introduce the chapter, title, and topics.

Help students identify important aspects of the chapter you are studying. For example, these might be:

- CrossQuotes

- CrossSeekers icons

- Highlighted material which indicates interactive opportunities with other students

- Opportunities for each student to express himself/herself in each chapter

- An awareness of the spiritual journey involved in the study each week

- Prayer of commitment after each chapter

Close the study each week with a time of prayer requests and prayer.

CHAPTER 1

Earnestly Seeking the Cross?

Discussion Suggestions:

- As a group, examine the CrossQuotes. Discuss what the CrossQuotes mean to them in daily living.

- Examine the interactive sections (indicated by the shaded background). How do they impact a student's lifestyle on campus?

- Ask, "What is your definition of "nonchalant Christianity?""

- What changes will students need to make in order to be CrossSeekers?

- How can other students be involved in the CrossSeekers movement on your campus?

CHAPTER 2

The Cross: The Expression of God's New Covenant

This chapter focuses on God's understanding of covenant living. Guide students to an understanding of how God's covenant can be a model for covenantal living in their lives.

Discussion Suggestions:

- What is the focus of God's covenant with man? How do you know?

- How can you guard against the symbol of God's covenant (the cross) becoming laissez-faire?

- After reading this chapter, who do you best identify with in the Bible related to covenantal living?

- What are the eight ways we can understand the meaning of the cross?

- How do the implications of the new covenant impact your life?. . .the lives of students?

- The statement is made, "When we choose to become CrossSeekers, we are making a total life-long commitment to know and experence Christ and to emulate Him as the Holy Spirit empowers us." Can you share your personal testimony with the students about how Christ impacts your life?

CHAPTER 3

The Cross: Exposing Contemporary Commitments

This chapter is designed to help students understand the contrast between the ways of Christ and the ways of the world. The Scripture is clear about the cost of being a seeker after the cross. What is not so clear is how the Christian principles of Christlike living intersect daily life on campus. What does it mean to "be not conformed to this world, but be transformed by the renewing of your mind?"

Discussion Suggestions:

- What is God's example of faithfulness? What difference does it make?

- What are the areas examined to offer the world's view of covenant?

- How does the fact that cheating on the college campus is on the rise make a difference in your life?

- Examine the section dealing with "Reflecting on the Cross and Our Commitments." Of these, which one or two should be priority for change in your life this coming week?

CHAPTER 4

Standing Before the Cross: A Crucified Life

The issues surrounding living a lifestyle of integrity are addressed in this chapter. For many students, integrity may be one of the hardest principles to grasp. Make sure time is allowed for students to discuss contemporary examples of the scriptural illustrations offered in this chapter. It should be a lively discussion.

Discussion Suggestions:

- The author asks, "How authentic a person of integrity are you?" He then offers three illustrations for authentic living from the Bible. Examine these illustrations. What would be contemporary collegiate situations for each illustration?

- How does the CrossQuote in this chapter speak directly to campus life?

- The author identifies nine areas of daily living which become a reality check for living a life of integrity. Which areas create the most concern for the participants?

- Is the issue of accountability important in order to live a lifestyle of Christian integrity?

CHAPTER 5

Taking Up Your Cross: Becoming Like Christ

How important is spiritual growth to a Christian? How can you identify a life growing spiritually? This chapter seeks to help the participant understand how depth of relationship with Christ will directly impact spiritual growth.

Discussion Suggestions:
- What are the three steps Jesus outlined for spiritual growth?

- How does wanting to do things your way get in God's way regarding your spiritual growth?

- Examine the CrossQuote in this chapter. Is this statement true? Why or why not?

- Look at the interactive section at the end of this chapter. If you were to graph your answers vertically, what would your graph look like?

CHAPTER 6

Carrying Your Cross Before Others: A Christlike Witness

What difference does it make to say you love someone? Does this mean you should be sharing this information with others? This chapter is designed to help participants understand the uniqueness of the message they have received from God about covenantal living and sharing one's faith.

Discussion Suggestions:
- Examine the CrossQuotes in this chapter. How do they help us understand commitment to share our faith with others?

- Examine the interactive questions concerning the importance of a love letter found early in the chapter. Which answers received the most checks? Why is this important?

- How would you have reacted to the woman at 33,000 feet?

- What are the three ways to witness according to the author?

- Is it important for a student to "write out" their personal testimony? Explain your answer.

- In the interactive section "Reflecting on Our Christian Witness," several questions are asked. How did the group do in answering these three questions?

- How important is the "Prayer of Commitment" for this chapter?

CHAPTER 7

The Attitude of the Cross: Giving Your Life for Others

Who has time for service? What is service all about? Why is service so important if you want to be a CrossSeeker? This chapter examines the principle of service and how it directs a CrossSeeker's journey. The good news in this chapter is that Christ has already demonstrated the direction for our journey of service.

Discussion Suggestions:
- How does the illustration with Norman Schwarzkopf deal with the principle of service for the CrossSeeker?

- As the author leads you to examine the scriptural basis for service, he identifies several areas where service can be demonstrated. Which of these areas are easiest for you to implement in your life? Which are hardest?

- Can you come up with a group statement to explain the importance of service for a CrossSeeker's life?

- The author says, "Your service as a CrossSeeker and a Christian is your monument to glorify God." What does this mean?

CHAPTER 8

Purified by the Cross

This chapter is about more than sexual purity. With this statement, a group of students begins examining why "purity" is one of the principles of authentic Christian living for the CrossSeeker. Is purity for a CrossSeeker more than sexual purity?

Discussion Suggestions:
- Can you name some of the moral blemishes on society today? What are they?

- CrossQuotes appear several times in this chapter. What significance do they represent for the CrossSeeker dealing with the issue of purity?

- Earlier, the issue of accountability was addressed under the principle of integrity. How might a group of students desiring to be CrossSeekers hold each other accountable for purity in their lifestyle?

CHAPTER 9

Relationships: Transformed by the Cross

How easy it is to throw a drink cup out the window of the car when we are through with it? How easy it is to think about buying a different vehicle when the car we have begins having problems? What if relationships were like the drinking cup or a broken down car, to be disposed of at will? Christ demonstrates in this chapter how important it is to develop Christlike relationships. Read on!

Discussion Suggestions:
- As you examine the sections in this chapter entitled, "In The News," how important would you say relationships

are to many who do not know the love of Christ? How does one deal with this day by day?

- Examine the CrossQuote about Jesus and his mother. Why did Jesus consider it important for us to be connected to our families?

- "Loving Our Enemies" is a section touching on those on campus we really don't spend much time with. Do you expect those you don't like to feel they should be treated in a Christlike manner as they deal with you? Why or why not?

- Can you pray the prayer of commitment?

OVERVIEW FOR THE CROSSSEEKER

- Go back to the first of the book and examine the CrossSeekers Covenant. Now that you have examined each principle of the Covenant through this study, how is your life different?

- Would you like to be a CrossSeeker? Talk to a religious leader on campus or in the church who can help you understand what your commitment to Jesus Christ is all about.

- CrossSeekers is a student led movement! Take it to your campus every day!

Covenant Resources

To order any of these resources, call toll free 1-800-458-2772.

Followology @ Collegiate Ministry: Following Jesus in the Real World
by Allen Jackson
Through an informal, interactive study, learn to follow the One who knows the way, because He *is* the Way!
ISBN 07673 9083 0 • *$9.95*

CROSS SEEKERS

---

will pursue consistent spiritual growth.
God's Invitation: A Challenge to College Students
by Henry Blackaby & Richard Blackaby
Through an interactive study focusing on application of the principles found in *Experiencing God*, students learn how these principles radically impact the daily issues of collegiate life. Seven sessions, 35 individual Bible studies.
ISBN 08054 9679 3 • *$9.95*

will speak and live a relevant, authentic, and consistent witness.
Into Their Shoes: Helping the Lost Find Christ
by John Kramp & Allen Jackson
By seeing life as non-believers do, collegians are challenged to move from confrontational gospel showdowns to relational in-their-shoes empathy. Each session includes interactive Bible study and group exercises. Helpful teaching suggestions are included for leaders.
ISBN 08054 9769 2 • *$9.95*

I will be godly in all things, Christlike in all relationships.
Discover the Winning Edge
by William Mitchell & Jerry Pounds
Through interactive study of six proven principles for developing godly self-esteem, students are challenged to develop positive habits, overcome fears, set goals, and rely on the strength Christ provides to discover the winning edge in life.
ISBN 07673 3178 8 • *$9.95*

I will be a person of integrity.
Out of the Moral Maze: Setting You Free to Make Right Choices
by Josh McDowell
Through group sessions and individual activities, students learn truth to apply to every moral dilemma of life. Workbook includes all teaching materials. ISBN 08054 9832 X • *$11.95*

I will honor my body as the temple of God, dedicated to a lifestyle of purity.
Faithful and True: Sexual Integrity in a Fallen World
by Mark R. Laaser
Where in our culture does a person go to develop a healthy and Christ-honoring attitude and lifestyle concerning sexuality? How can Christians and the church respond to a world gone sexually mad? This book seeks to answer these questions. ISBN 08054 9819 2 • *$12.95*

I will seek opportunities to serve in Christ's name.
Meeting Needs, Sharing Christ: Ministry Evangelism in Today's New Testament Church
by Don Atkinson and Charles Roesel
Leads individuals and churches to understand the concept and capture the vision for ministry evangelism, identify needs, and minister to broken lives in the community. Six-week small-group study.
ISBN 08054 9840 0 • *$6.95*

Leader's Guide
ISBN 08054 9841 9
• *$6.95*

Transitions: Preparing for College
compiled by Art Herron
Designed for the high school junior/senior preparing for college. Written to answer many questions you may have about college...and how to begin the process of becoming a CrossSeeker in your junior/senior years. Practical helps such as the "time line" keep you on track.
ISBN 07673 9082 2 • *$7.95* (Student Version)

To order any of these resources, call toll free 1-800-458-2772.

Covenant Resources
To order any of these resources,
call toll free 1-800-458-2772.

INTEGRITY

CrossSeekers: Transparent Living
by Rod Handley
Living a life of integrity can be difficult. Accountability groups provide a support system, enabling collegians to help one another stay on track. *CrossSeekers: Transparent Living* provides a biblical study of living with integrity and guidance for staying accountable for your integrity through an accountability group. (6 sessions) •*$6.95 Available 11/98*

CHRISTLIKE
RELATIONSHIPS

CrossSeekers: Soul Food for Relationships
by J. Keith Miller
Our relationships with other people are key to happiness and success in life. Too often, though, these relationships become strained, stressful. How can we keep them Christlike? J. Keith Miller examines the false soul or personality we create that leaves us feeling lonely, fearful, doubtful. Confronting this constructed soul and dismantling the self-created aspects lead us to authentic living and Christlike relationships.
(6 sessions) • *$6.95 Available 12/98*

SPIRITUAL
GROWTH

CrossSeekers: Spiritual Intimacy
by Glen Martin and Dian Ginter
A resource to intensify the desire of your heart to know God more intimately, help you realize where you are in the process of getting closer to God, and show you how to move ahead by knowing God on six successive levels.
(6 sessions) • *$6.95 Available 1/99*

PURITY

CrossSeekers: Holy and Acceptable
First Corinthians 6 tells us that our bodies are temples of the Holy Spirit. But what does that mean, and why should we care? This study looks at what it means for us to be God's temple. Through Bible study and contemporary situations, the physical, mental, and spiritual aspects are explored, along with their inter-relatedness, as well as what to do when you fail in your pursuit of purity. (6 sessions) • *$6.95 Available 4/99*

For the latest in student resources, visit the CrossSeekers Web site
www.crossseekers.com